LEADING LADIES

LEADING LADIES

TEXT BY DON MACPHERSON
DESIGN BY LOUISE BRODY

FOREWORD BY RICHARD SCHICKEL

PHOTOGRAPHS FROM
THE KOBAL COLLECTION

ST. MARTIN'S PRESS
NEW YORK

First published in 1986 by
Conran Octopus Limited
28-32 Shelton Street
London WC2 9PH

First U.S. Edition
10 9 8 7 6 5 4 3 2 1

Printed and bound in Spain

Frontispiece: studio portrait of Katharine Hepburn, 1935.
Photographer Ernest A. Bachrach.
Overleaf: Joan Crawford signing publicity photographs, 1934.

Acknowledgments The publishers would like to thank the following film distribution and
production companies whose film stills and publicity portraits appear in this book: A.F.E.,
Cocinor, Columbia, Embassy, EMI, Gaumont, Janus, Ladd Company, Lux, MGM, NBC, New
World, Paramount, Pathé, Rank, Republic, RKO, Selznick International, SNC, Speva,
Svenskfilmindustri, Titanus, 20th Century Fox, United Artists, Universal, Warner Brothers.

Library of Congress Cataloging in Publication Data

Macpherson, Don.
    Leading ladies.

        1. Moving-pictures actors and actresses—
United States.   I. Title.
PN1998.A2M267   1986   791.43'028'0922   86-13833
ISBN 0-312-47649-3

CONTENTS

FOREWORD 7

INTRODUCTION 8

THE SILENT ERA 12

THE CLASSICS 32

THE NEO-CLASSICS 108

THE 'NEW LOOK' 162

MODERN TIMES 196

INDEX 224

FOREWORD

Gathered in these pages in dazzling plenitude are the dreamworks of some seven decades. At a superficial level these years represent the better part of a century, but in a more complex sense the images also represent the *better* part of a century that has, on the whole, very few good parts.

We know, of course, that these images would not exist if their flesh and blood subjects had not given the cameras something to fawn upon and then re-create according to the commercial and erotic values of the time. But of such mundane matters we never wanted to think and, as the years wear on, we care to contemplate them even less. One never thought of these women having the sniffles or being prey to black humours (though, since they were actresses, it was tolerable to imagine them as capable of red-hot tantrums). Nor did one care to think about the manipulation that they were subjected to by their employers even though, when the studios were at the height of their power and these women were often bound to them by long-term contract, there was no lack of comment on this point. But this was merely an inconvenient reality, something to escape as quickly and as often as one could, and it was the function of these photographs to facilitate that process. Their considerable art lay in capturing, in a still and silent studio portrait, the erotic essence that a star projected in her films. If anything, the photographs were more highly stylized than any of those moving pictures. Their limitations were, of course, their strengths. There were no distractions here — no plot, no co-stars, no exotic settings or highly-charged action sequences to compete with the star for our attention. There was only this delicious object, perfectly gowned, coiffed and made-up and, above all, artfully lit, for us to comtemplate for as long as we chose to do so and in a time and place that suited us.

We could make of her what we would — someone to emulate if we were women, possess in our imaginations if we were men. Or, if not that, turn her into an ideal, annunciation of which announced something about ourselves to those with whom — very choosily — we shared our deeper secrets.

Potent stuff, obviously. Just how potent we did not know at the time. It is only as the years go by and we encounter anew — as in a book like this — the images that informed our adolescence, that we find ourselves astonished by the afterlife of something that was created for the expedient, even crass, purposes of publicity. We find ourselves yet more astonished by their power to evoke not just the movies of times gone by, but something of the social history of that period and of our own half-forgotten lives as well.

The photographs contained in *Leading Ladies* are possibly not dreamworks as psychology employs the term — too much conscious calculation, too much artfulness has gone into their creation. But they assuredly became the basis for a part of almost everyone's daydreams. No matter what decade of this century contained your impressionable years as a movie-goer, some part of your past will be returned to you in these pages. It may puzzle you or please you; it may provoke wry or wistful feelings. You may care to share those feelings or hold them in strictest confidence, but you will recognize that they are of no small consequence.

RICHARD SCHICKEL

INTRODUCTION

'The truth about me is . . .
that nothing written about me is true . . .'
Marlene Dietrich

Once upon a time, movie stars used to belong in movie theatres. Occasionally, of course, they could be glimpsed on a billboard, in a fan magazine, a newspaper snippet or a newsreel. But mostly they appeared in their rightful place – on the movie screen – within a sumptuously decorated holy of holies in which congregations gathered by their millions. It was no surprise that cinemas came to resemble secular temples, decked out in thick velvet and gleaming in flickering light. For movie stars became the closest thing to gods or goddesses that audiences ever saw: giant shadows of sombre beauty and entrancing smiles, locked in battles and embraces more powerful or passionate than humans could imagine. But that, of course, was all once upon a time.

Nowadays movie stars seem to belong anywhere *but* movie theatres. Out on the streets are billboards of Jean Harlow advertising matches; on television a clip from an old Barbara Stanwyck movie is used to sell lager; in the bookshops a novel called *Betrayed By Rita Hayworth*, a book of short stories called *Mae West is Dead*, or a bizarre hybrid of Hollywood fact and fiction called *Suspects*, are all for sale. In the Sunday papers, there is a choice of reading about Joan Crawford's 1920s porno pictures, Cecil Beaton's account of his love affair with Greta Garbo, or the latest attempt to unravel the mysterious death of Marilyn Monroe. If this gets too much, perhaps a visit to the theatre for a new play about Judy Garland; to the art gallery for an exhibition of photographic portraits with Vivien Leigh on the poster; or a quiet evening at home watching the re-runs of Marlene Dietrich movies on television.

The process has been happening slowly over thirty years. Movie stars have proliferated and spread like viruses ever since television began to purchase Hollywood's back catalogue of movies in the late fifties.

Television's 'The Late Show' was a beacon which lit a ghostly eternal flame for stars whose brightness was long ago eclipsed. Movies which had slipped from sight were resurrected like celluloid Frankensteins, and stars from the 1930s and 1940s reached not only their old audiences again, but also a generation of new admirers. Strange things began to happen. Cults began to form around stars like Harlow, Garbo, Mae West or Joan Crawford, who had all slipped from popularity. For many the appreciation was on a level of 'camp' or ironic detachment, spoofing the manner and styles of a former era; in others there was genuine affection for stars who seemed once again a novelty. When Andy Warhol made silkscreen prints of Marilyn Monroe in the early sixties, she joined the ranks of Elvis Presley and Jackie Kennedy as one of those icons of 'pop life' who were to become as ubiquitous as the logo for a Brillo pad. Movie stars had truly entered the democratic era; they no longer belonged to a remote holy of holies, but to a new supermarket of images.

They could appear, literally, anywhere; and in the mid-sixties they did. Jean Harlow's likeness appeared on a pair of tights; Clara Bow, the 'It' girl, gazed out from an underground newspaper; Theda Bara, the World War One vamp, turned up on a toilet roll holder, while Dietrich and Garbo were glimpsed on T-shirts, tissues and sweatshirts. Sometimes they even appeared in revivals of their own movies. But there was still developing a peculiar kind of fascination with these stars. It was at once casual yet obsessive, careless yet devoted. The nostalgic guessing game 'Whatever Happened To . . .?' became the token of concern for stars who someone, somewhere, had once loved.

If this is an era of high-tech cannibalism, it's not surprising if things get a little out of hand. Two recent movies, *The Lady In Red* and *Insignificance*, both use the old Marilyn Monroe poster shot where her dress is lifted up by a gust of wind, satisfying with one quotation our urge to conjure integrity by associating the offerings of today with tried and tested images from yesterday. This post-modernist age is at least consistent – but then perhaps it's nothing new. Didn't Monroe herself base her style upon Lana Turner? And didn't Turner base herself on Jean Harlow? What *is* new is that cinema audiences can be relied upon to recognize the shot, even if they've never seen *The Seven Year Itch* whence it came. The point is that the original has long since disappeared. All that remains are the traces of adjustments and refinements that have occurred over the decades. And in this book, as you turn the pages, those shifts and alterations will slowly become visible.

The title of the book itself belongs to a bygone age. The term 'Leading Ladies' suggests gentility and sensuality, sophistication, glamour and politeness – not qualities intrinsic to the present. It properly belongs to an era which passed some thirty years ago, and which had lasted for some thirty years before that. Between 1920 and 1950 the cinema was the great arbiter of who would become our leading ladies. This was the period during which the combination of an industrial system (of movie production, contracts, publicity and distribution) and the confidence of a rising nation – the United States of America – brought a unique collection of leading ladies into existence.

America, and, of course, the small west-coast town of Hollywood, became the dream of every romantic boy and girl – or at least of those who were poor, tired or hungry; Hollywood's glamour dominated foreign film industries. During the 1920s and early 1930s women came from all over the USA, from Sweden, Germany, France and occasionally Britain for a chance of stardom. They were a mixed bunch, daughters of labourers, (Garbo), dentists (Harlow), bank managers (Shirley Temple) and boxers (Mae West), who once earned crusts as small-town shopgirls, chorus girls, drama students or even actresses before being fashioned into movie stars. The time-honoured route was via a beauty contest win or a dance competition, with the first prize a trip to Hollywood. These lucky few were seen simultaneously as actresses and potential goddesses, as both real-life women and industrial commodities to be styled and fashioned to the standards of a Detroit automobile or a Ming vase.

Joan Crawford, for example, persistently changed her hairstyle, lipstick, eye make-up and then her whole look to adapt to passing trends that she was adamant would not leave her behind. Jean Harlow was transformed from a Kansas girl to a Popcorn Venus by a process of eyebrow plucking and hair realignment which made her former self virtually unrecognizable. In all these changes, the stars remodelled their homely good looks to become ideals of beauty. Governed by the whims of MGM's Louis B. Mayer or Columbia's Harry Cohn, these leading ladies were to be living symbols of a nation's new ideals of womanhood. Whatever insecurities surfaced during this turbulent period of history, the stars never wavered in their appeal to everyone from the Idaho farmer to the Chicago bartender.

Not forgotten among the audiences were, of course, the millions of independent young women who had flocked to the big cities after the First World War to take advantage of automation, office work, shops and personal services. A new generation of typists, shopgirls, waitresses, manicurists, taxi-dancers, clerks, usherettes and more lived out their dreams through Hollywood's newly realistic heroines who, like Colleen Moore or Clara Bow, apparently lived lives like their own, and suffered the slings and arrows of romance with unaccustomed vigour and pzazz.

But in its strictest sense, a leading lady was more than a romantic star. She was an actress whose name appeared above the movie title on a marquee, and usually opposite only one other name – that of her male co-star. A leading lady carried the movie's principal female interest alone. She was obviously supported by character actresses, rivals, bit-players or chorus girls; but essentially a leading lady was teamed romantically with a leading man. So an audience would expect to see how Bette Davis, Katharine Hepburn or Olivia De Havilland fared with a man, whether it was Cary Grant, Clark Gable or Errol Flynn. But 'leading lady' was not just a cute synonym for a leading female star. It was a term of public acclaim, and of legal and contractual seriousness. Actresses could be stars without necessarily being able to be leading ladies, as Dietrich discovered in the late 1930s, or Ginger Rogers discovered after leaving Fred Astaire. The accolade of leading lady was not just important from vanity's point of view. It indicated both studio confidence and the size of a pay-cheque.

Who was – and who was not – a leading lady reflected many things, with acting ability a relatively minor consideration. A gap in a studio's ranks of players might lift an unknown bit-player into romantic roles, or competition with another studio's star might briefly cause a rash of Garbos or Harlows. But aside from acting skill or studio fickleness, the crucial factor was the ability to reflect truthfully the broad sweep of social aspirations, to promise fulfilment of the dreams and desires of the movie audiences, and to produce customers who paid dollars and cents for tickets for the big feature.

Before World War One the screen was filled with Victorian icons or Pre-Raphaelite beauties with long flowing hair. The 'Pollyanna' character of Mary Pickford and the disarming purity of Lillian Gish were both variations on Victorian types, distilled through the voluminous moral literature of the period from a range of sources including Bible picture books, popular folk tales and fairy stories. To Pickford's Cinderella, the vamp Theda Bara was a picture-book Jezebel, a veritable she-devil who wrecked homes and set sin at the family's door. There was a big jump from these mythical icons to the bold series of comedies and melodramas directed by Cecil B. DeMille, in which Gloria Swanson embodied a more modern woman to whom marriage was a temporary state of affairs, divorce an inconvenience, and adultery a sport. This pragmatic and hedonistic style paved the way for stars such as Pola Negri, Alla Nazimova and Garbo herself, whose exotic and passionate charisma was a matter for approval and envy rather than moral distaste.

The 'jazz babies' of the Roaring Twenties, like Colleen Moore and Clara Bow, catered for a lower, though no less hedonistic, stratum of society. The new styles of heroine were supposed to resemble millions of big city girls. They were 'dames', 'broads', opportunistic 'gold diggers', or they were 'flappers' – the girls who lived for the moment and danced all night at the wild weekends of Prohibition parties.

But just as the First World War had made certain old-fashioned attitudes perish, the Great Crash of 1929 and Depression of the 1930s had a withering effect on the jazz babies, and sound killed off many a silent star. During the 1930s, as the dream factory slipped into gear, a great variety of new attitudes were required. MGM stars like Garbo, Shearer, Harlow and Crawford glitzed through sumptuous displays of drawing-room elegance – but now there was also Myrna Loy's portrait of married bliss with William Powell, or there was the screwball craziness of Lombard, Hepburn and others, while at Warners Bette Davis brought a new melodramatic realism into vogue. Censorship grew stricter in the mid-thirties, and risqué performers like Mae West and Jean Harlow had to clean up their acts as propriety began to prevail.

A new series of archetypes replaced those of the Biblical picture books and fairy stories. These drew instead on the movies' own iconography and plotlines, and the role of the exotic outsider shifted from Garbo's shoulders to Hedy Lamarr's and then to Ingrid Bergman's, while that of the platinum blonde shifted from Harlow's to Veronica Lake's to Lana Turner's. These new archetypes were drawn from the developing genres of gangster movie, screwball comedy, melodrama or mystery, and reflected a growing confidence in American social types and institutions: the exotic temptress or goddess vied with the wise-cracking dame or the perfect wife; the strong woman competed with the blonde bombshell or society lady. Success in any one of these roles brought consolidation and typecasting.

Until the Second World War, when leading ladies varied between the extremes of the lonely wife and the Vargas-style pin-up, there was little seen of the new, urban femme fatale, those disruptive, unknowable, brooding and passionate women who could trounce their weak leading men like Alan Ladd, Dana Andrews and Glenn Ford. Their vogue came in the later forties. Such ambiguity and ambivalence about male and female sexuality was then cancelled in the transition to the peaceful Eisenhower years of family life and suburban dreams; busty fifties leading ladies stressed a new security, perhaps as postponed relief from wartime neuroses and flaws.

But the rise of television and pop music had begun to produce a constant stream of stars, and these rival industries were more capable than the studios of responding quickly to public taste and styles. By the late fifties the Hollywood cinema became a splendidly grand anachronism, out of touch with changing social habits and fashions. The leading role taken by Hollywood in the twenties, thirties and forties in establishing new trends and archetypes had been surrendered, and cinema of the Hollywood style was now synonymous with an old-fashioned view of the world. Indeed the very success of creating female stereotypes and role models which had influenced the world came to be seen with increasing scepticism, then cynicism and eventually downright hostility.

The mid-sixties then brought a vogue for anti-Hollywoodism, in which behaviour and attitude became as loose and unstructured as possible, while glamour became a symbol of unthinking conformity. In this modern attitude, the very concept of a 'leading lady' became an irrelevance and an outmoded reminder of a Hollywood system which had seemingly been both defeated and forgotten. But after the euphoria of the late sixties a period of consolidation and settlement occurred, until it seemed that Hollywood might yet be forgiven. As if symbolically, Jane Fonda at last did just that in the early 1980s.

Always the most modern attitudes seem pragmatic and ironic, perhaps willing to learn lessons from the past, but prepared also to rubbish the precepts of a previous age. The social and mythical status which was accorded to a Garbo, Harlow or Dietrich no longer operates for Kathleen Turner, Rosanna Arquette or Michelle Pfeiffer; these stars can be talked of as leading ladies in a movie, but not outside. The burden of myth has shifted more towards pop stars like Madonna, herself a crazed mixture of Marilyn Monroe and Minnie Mouse. The past, it seems, no longer bears down as heavily as it once did; the style of Dietrich, Harlow, Veronica Lake or Rita Hayworth no longer seems either as oppressive or as unreachable as it once did, but instead has become an archive from which bits and pieces can be stolen and refashioned into something new and possibly contradictory.

For this is the age of cut-ups, where the past is an open arena from which parts which please can be lifted and adapted. In the age of the video rewind, of the magazine, the movie book, the postcard, all past glories are available for inspection at the flick of a switch. Our modern attitude is markedly different from the nostalgia of the sixties, which welcomed a Harlow or a Bara silhouette in simple-minded rediscovery, or the more camp attitude of the seventies, which struck poses of a Bette Davis, Joan Crawford or Mae West with knowing irony. For the modern attitude is marked by its self-consciousness, its knowledge of arcane areas of trivia and detail, its disregard for previous patterns of order and rank; we believe ourselves free to make of the past what we want, without reference to previous interpretations or styles.

We cannot measure the richness which we owe to movie stars such as Garbo, Dietrich, Hepburn, Davis or Gish. They seem too firmly imprinted on modern memories for their images to be quickly erased. They are symbols of celebrity in a culture increasingly devoted to the worship of fame itself. In retrospect, it is easy to forget how recent is the entire phenomenon. For it is merely seventy-five years since the first actresses began to be known by name in the movies, and many of the most exalted celluloid goddesses are still alive. The illusion of divinity is perhaps difficult to reconcile with the sight of a reclusive Garbo still shooing away pestering photographers in Manhattan, of Lillian Gish stepping on to a stage to deliver a speech on one of her early movies, or with a brief glimpse of Dietrich through a telefoto lense. Or is it more true that we make almost no connection between the gorgeous icon we can still see on film, and an old lady snapped by a press photographer? They are in truth different beings.

All these actresses, and those of their generation, grew up in a period when cinema was still writing its rules and conditions; when America was still aspiring to a yearned-for position of greatness; and when the movies were the world's prime medium of excitement and romance. The performances of many of those actresses reveal in their passion that they had everything to live for. Despite the studio bosses, and the indignities of the star system, a gallery of romantic lovers and adventurous heroines was formed which has become the basis for the dream-lives of future generations. Just as *A Thousand and One Nights* was filmed over and over again in cinema's early days, the movies' own stories and leading ladies form the popular folk tales and myths of the next century. Those heroines may now appear as little more than a flickering black-and-white image turned up at random from all the thousands available, but their spell is still undeniable. Next time one of their movies appears on television, just pause for a moment — consider how rich and exciting their contribution has been.

THE SILENT ERA

The leading ladies of silent movies often have a curious pedigree. For before cinema established its own rules for stardom, the gallery of faces that appeared on the flickering screen was taken from a bizarre range of influences. American audiences, comprised of immigrants from Poland, Italy, Sweden, Ireland, Russia or Central Europe, may not have been able to understand one another; but they came to understand the movies because Mary Pickford, 'The Girl With The Golden Curls', was in their minds Pollyanna or Cinderella, or Theda Bara was the Jezebel or Delilah they'd seen in their Bible picture books. The earliest generation of cinemagoers was often illiterate, speaking a veritable Babel of languages, so common folk myths were ransacked for ideas. The Bible was a principal source, while children's fairy tales, from Hansel and Gretel to Snow White, blended with exotic tales from the Arabian Nights, Pre-Raphaelite paintings, Victorian 'improvement' literature, vaudeville, literary classics and tales of the early pioneers. If audiences wanted titillation by the thought of 'Flesh and the Devil' or 'Women of Sin' they also got the moral chastisement that went with it. Not until the jazz babies and 'It' girls of the 1920s, the gun molls and loose women of Clara Bow, Colleen Moore or Evelyn Brent, did recognizably new types make their debut; and even then, the countless remakes of *Salome, Cleopatra, Madame Du Barry, Camille, Romeo and Juliet*, and *Anna Karenina* continued.

But even in the earliest Kinetoscope arcades, the lines of squat, wooden peep-show cabinets that preceded the nickelodeon theatres, one romantic topic proved ripe for endless variations: The Kiss. Among the earliest 'flickers' of waves lapping on a seashore, of tall blondes raising their skirts, or of skits on women's right to vote, *The Kiss* was a favourite. In 1896 Edison had released a version of a middle-aged embrace which proved as scandalworthy as the same firm's lewd display of a Coney Island belly-dancer. By 1903 a whole series called *The Kiss* featured 'leading exponents of the art of artistical embraces' – already there were specialists in romantic scenes of illicit love. How to show kissing, how to match the right actor and actress, how to thread a story around a mildly erotic embrace became, in one sense, the secret chemistry of making successful movies. The task was simple, yet capable of a thousand variations and sophistications, and it reached its culmination when Greta Garbo starred in MGM's *The Kiss* in 1929, during the last months of the silent era.

By then something crucial had happened. In less than thirty years, 'the crown and flower of nineteenth century magic' – as one comment on early cinema had it – had been converted into hard cash, real estate, and America's fifth largest industry. By the end of the 1920s cinema consisted of over twenty thousand theatres with audiences of one hundred million people every week. The sleepy west-coast town of Hollywood had boomed into a Babylonian metropolis.

Carving out fortunes and territories between 1910 and the mid-1920s was almost as fraught and bloody a process as the gang wars of this Prohibition era. A series of anti-Trust legal cases had restricted some corporate abuses, but sharp practices such as block-booking movies into cinemas were still a much-resented staple of studio activity. For studios established rigid control as protection against both the fickleness of the masses and the demands of the bankers. And one of the greatest weapons in the moguls' armoury was the star system.

Actors and actresses had initially remained anonymous, since the studios feared that fame would arouse demands for higher salaries. Stars were known only by their company names ('The Biograph girl', 'The IMP girl', 'The Vitagraph girl') or screen types ('Little Mary', or 'The Waif'). But in 1910 Carl Laemmle, then at IMP, audaciously poached 'the Biograph Girl' and revealed her to be Florence Lawrence. He organized a huge publicity campaign around her, boosting her salary from $25 to $1,000 a week; and public interest proved insatiable. A demand was soon spotted for information on these real-life heroines. By 1912 fan magazines began to cater for twenty million regular moviegoers, and by 1913 most major companies had publicity departments to promote such interest – by fair means or foul. From then on, 'leading ladies' could be created from thin air. A ruse by William Fox in 1914 transformed the stage actress Theodosia de Coppet into the exotic vamp Theda Bara, while fame guaranteed Mary Pickford's success in negotiating a salary increase from a few hundred dollars per week in 1914 to $350,000 per picture by 1917. Pickford retained independent control of her career, but Bara was the first of many unfortunates who found herself bound by the almost feudal terms of her contract with Fox. After her success had peaked in 1919, she was discarded without conscience or care for her future.

The vamp had been a primitive caricature, a bold, Bible-based type of Jezebel, who went out of fashion after World War One, just as Bara's own heavy black make-up became out of touch with the new everyday styles brought into fashion by the emerging beauty salons and cosmetic industries of Helena Rubenstein or Elizabeth Arden. For in the social upheavals following 1918, the Victorian sentimentality of Mary Pickford, the Gish sisters or Bara was brushed aside. Pious notions that poverty is next to godliness, or that a sound marriage is the bedrock of a woman's joy, were mocked by a new and sophisticated middle-class cinema audience. Instead of Cinderella or Pollyanna's home-sweet-home, the movies shifted their attention to an upwardly mobile world of luxurious apartments, electrically-fitted kitchens and sleek automobiles, symbols of a hedonistic nation surfing on a wave of prosperity.

Kissing was no longer regarded as the first sign of the devil but more as a flirtatious sport; and the bustle and the waltz were replaced by the flapper skirt and the Charleston. Pepped-up jazz babies like Colleen Moore, Clara Bow, Joan Crawford or Louise Brooks inhabited a brave new world in which a career choice as wife, domestic servant or prostitute had blossomed into a myriad of new – if lowly – jobs in the expanding cities. New movie heroines were shopgirls, typists, clerks, manicurists, taxi-dancers, chorus girls or secretaries.

They were go-getting, fun-loving creatures aspiring to the silk stockings and underwear of the next rung of heroines: the slender sophisticates such as Gloria Swanson or Norma Shearer, the exotics like Greta Garbo, Pola Negri or Vilma Banky.

Coyness about romance and sexual attraction had been superceded by a seductive eroticism, evident in movies by Cecil B. DeMille, Erich von Stroheim and Ernst Lubitsch. In *Male and Female*, 1919, *Foolish Wives*, 1922, or *Forbidden Paradise*, 1924, divorce was a pragmatic affair, sin was a sport, and nightclubs were more suitable haunts for women than the kitchen.

Hollywood's thrills of 'speed, spice and spectacle' still caused outrage. The scandal that destroyed comedian Fatty Arbuckle's career in 1921 after a wild weekend of booze, drugs and women sparked a national moral panic that precipitated censorship of movies' content. For if the twenties saw the rise of speakeasies, bathing beauties, crossword puzzles, real-life Lindberghs and fictional Jay Gatsbys, then the background to this carefree playground was nationwide political, religious and racial intolerance. It was a period of rabid anti-Communism, one that saw the growth of the Ku Klux Klan and the rise of fervent religious evangelism that joined spiritual battle for the soul of America. Hollywood's liberal doses of flesh and the devil were often seen to be as corrupting as the demon alcohol. DeMille became a canny judge of public taste, and his *The Ten Commandments*, 1923, managed to portray both ample visual sinful delights *and* the longed-for divine retribution. Such compromises became a constant formula in the next decade.

The vast changes that took place during thirty years of silents can be exemplified by a movie like *Sunrise*, 1927, one of the three movies for which Janet Gaynor won the first Academy Award. Our hero George O'Brien plots to kill his sweet wife (Gaynor) because he has fallen in love with a vamp and is drawn to the bright lights of the big city. We are shown the sexy vamp in silken clothes and make-up, and we see the thrills of the huge metropolis, but in a heart-breaking series of scenes the hero goes back to Gaynor and a life of rural simplicity sweetened by experience. It is a timeless story which incorporates old-fashioned elements of fairy-tale romance, Gaynor's very individual style of acting, and director F. W. Murnau's sophisticated story-telling techniques, and blends them with moving cameras, complex images and a bold narrative style. Its silence is eloquent and breathtakingly modern, a confident statement of the abilities of the now established cinema.

THEDA BARA

Theda Bara appeared like a thunderbolt in a world where marriage was an inviolate sanctuary, and the relationship between husbands and wives supposed to be sober and straitlaced. With her dark, flashing eyes and flowing hair, she was a compelling choice for the screen's first 'vamp': a threatening, other-worldly figure robed in muslin, jewels and feathers, who would toss back her head and laugh at her unfortunate lover's destruction. Her first starring role, *A Fool There Was*, 1915, was a heady brew of sinful melodrama concocted by the young William Fox. It set this twenty-five-year-old actress firmly in the American public's fevered imagination as a

mysterious she-devil, while Fox's razzamatazz proclaimed her to be the offspring of a sheik and a princess, her name an anagram of ARAB DEATH.

She was like a living illustration of 'Sin' from a child's Bible picture-book, and she appealed to a growing middle-class audience for whom the sophistications of the love triangle were of enormous interest. In more than thirty-five films made over five years, Bara played Salome, Camille, Madame Du Barry and Cleopatra, creating a repertoire of archetypal temptresses copied by succeeding generations. Bara's image was the evil and erotic 'Dark Angel of Destiny', hair falling languorously over bare shoulders, breasts

cupped by gilded serpents. It seemed to matter little that in reality the heroine of *Tiger Woman*, *Purgatory*, *Eternal Sin* and *Sin*, all 1914-1919, was a tailor's daughter from Ohio, christened Theodosia Goodman.

By 1919 the vogue for man-eating vampires was over. Fox, his company now firmly established thanks to Bara, had no more use for her. She was left as an almost unemployable legend, the first leading lady offered up on a plate for her sexual allure and then callously discarded.

ABOVE: publicity portrait for *Cleopatra*, 1917. Photographer Witzel
OPPOSITE: publicity portrait for *Salome*, 1918. Photographer Witzel

EVELYN BRENT

Although she had starred opposite John Barrymore as early as 1917 in *Raffles the Amateur Cracksman*, Evelyn Brent's finest moments came late in the 1920s. For director Josef von Sternberg, later to be Dietrich's mentor, she made three films: *Underworld*, 1927, its follow-up *The Dragnet*, and the Academy Award winning vehicle for Emil Jannings, *The Last Command*, both 1928. In *Underworld* Brent incarnated the figure of the gun moll with her role as Feathers McCoy in the first hit of Hollywood's gangster cycle. Her character marked a break from the heroines and villainesses of the silent era: Feathers McCoy was distinct from the vampish, smouldering parts Brent was used to playing. Here was a tough and pragmatic contemporary heroine caught up in the Chicago scene, the sidekick of a ruthless gangster (George Bancroft), who falls in love with his best friend, a suave lawyer played by Clive Brook. Dressed in a feather boa and more gaudy get-ups, Brent is torn between two lovers during a final shoot-out, her dilemma intensified by the machine-gun bullets zipping around her head. Feathers McCoy is, of course, a figure snatched from the headlines by journalist Ben Hecht and flung on to the screen; but it was a transitional role, part expressionistic fantasy and part hard-boiled realism, and a worthy prototype for those hard-headed 'dames' of the early 1930s when gun molls started to talk. Brent herself slid easily into the talkies, and didn't make her last film until 1948.

ABOVE: *Underworld*, 1927, with Clive Brook

Pola Negri knew her public well. She appeared at Valentino's funeral dressed in widow's clothes, worth $13,000 according to the publicity; distraught with emotion and propped up by her maid, she screamed with grief, swooned, and, before an audience of thousands, fainted to the ground. It was a great performance by Valentino's last flame – the Queen of Paramount, and that studio's only rival to Swanson.

Descended from a gipsy family, so the story went, Negri studied ballet in St Petersburg, acted in Warsaw, and rose to fame in Berlin under the great impresarios Max Reinhardt and Ernst Lubitsch. One of her German films for Lubitsch, *Madame Dubarry*, 1918, was revamped as a big American hit under the title *Passion*. Her success brought her offers of Hollywood contracts, and she made her first film there in 1923.

In retrospect Negri's extravagant emotions and haughty disdain for screen lovers such as Conrad Nagel and Adolphe Menjou appear outrageously indulgent, but she was everything that prim middle-class American ladies were supposed not to be: passionate, unashamedly erotic, arrogant and remote. The audiences delighted in her brooding histrionics in films like *Vendetta*, 1921, *Medea*, 1921, *The Spanish Dancer*, 1923, and when she played the Tsarina of a small Russian state in Lubitsch's *Forbidden Paradise*, 1924.

But as her guises became ever more elaborate, from silks and draperies to batwinged capes and spiders' web collars, she turned into an affected parody of her former self. Her roles in *Hotel Imperial* and *Barbed Wire*, both 1927, were her last real hits of any stature, and she began to be overlooked now that a newer foreign import, Greta Garbo, was taking the limelight. She spent the 1930s in Germany as one of Hitler's favourites, but returned to the USA, and to the occasional character part, after the outbreak of the Second World War.

RIGHT: *Bella Donna*, 1923, with Macey Harlam

LILLIAN GISH

The Gish sisters were complementary and exceptionally hard-working actresses, learning their craft through exacting schedules and changing parts two or three times a week. Of the two, Dorothy was the slighter actress, a younger echo of Lillian, though both possessed that wispy frailty and freshness which was to prove so appealing. Dorothy kept up a long and successful film and stage career, but she was always eclipsed by her more ethereal sister and it is Lillian's name that appears under 'Gish' in the annals of cinema history.

Lillian is unjustly recognized as the paragon of simple, old-fashioned, nineteenth-century feminine virtue. D. W. Griffith saw her as a virgin of true heart, self-sacrificing and rather unexciting; and certainly her roles in *Hearts of the World*, 1918, *Broken Blossoms*,

True Heart Susie, both 1919, and *Orphans of the Storm*, 1921, are saturated with Griffith's brand of unctuous Victorian sentimentality. But the role which brought Gish worldwide fame — Elsie Stoneman in *Birth of a Nation*, 1915 — already seemed to speak of a bygone age.

For Lillian Gish was truly the first *modern* actress in cinema. Audiences loved her ability to suggest complex emotions directly to the camera. Here, for the first time, was an actress who was not merely untheatrical but positively cinematic. In some of the earliest close-ups she manages to project all the contradictions of a Pre-Raphaelite painting. Garlanded, virginal, she is also highly sensual, and she could suggest a devastating mix of vulnerable innocence and underlying passion. As a gentle Virginian girl who

murders an assailant in *The Wind*, 1928, Gish conveys emotions of fear and devotion as if for the first time, her face at once terrifying and exhilarating.

Contracted to MGM in 1925 for $8,000 a week, Gish made a series of fine pictures but fell foul of a studio publicity machine which saw her as overpaid and out of fashion. In Louise Brooks' words, she was 'stigmatized at the age of thirty-one as a grasping, silly, sexless antique', but after her departure from Hollywood in the late twenties, she maintained a highly successful stage career, punctuated by occasional character parts in cinema and television.

OPPOSITE: *The Wind*, 1928
ABOVE: *Orphans of the Storm*, 1921, with Dorothy Gish

MAE MURRAY

Mae Murray was 'The Girl with the Bee-Stung Lips', one of the most hedonistic of the rags-to-riches stars of the 1920s. A sultry-eyed blonde who abhorred the old-fashioned Pickfordian-sweetheart style, she leapt from Broadway and the Ziegfeld Follies into movies in 1916, starred with her friend Valentino in *The Delicious Little Devil*, 1919, and hoofed her way through *The Gilded Lily*, 1921, and *Jazzmania*, 1923, to emerge as a high-living super-star with a canary-yellow limousine and attendant chauffeur and hounds. As the star of Erich von Stroheim's *The Merry Widow*, 1925, she was the ob-ject of John Gilbert's lustful attentions, and after an on-set row with Stroheim she outraged middle America with her magazine revelations about 'The Dirtiest Hun in Hollywood'. Her riches-to-rags tumble was as meteoric as had been her rise. She divorced her third husband, director Robert Z. Leonard, and, like Swanson and Negri, married real-life royalty in the shape of Prince David Mdivani, and followed his counsel to quit her MGM contract. Such behaviour was not liked, and parts became difficult to come by. The Prince lost interest as her fortune dwindled. The talkies left Murray far behind, and, impoverished but with belief in her own status as a star resolutely intact, she drifted into obscurity. Stories of vagrancy, bankruptcy, the loss of custody of her son, all filtered through to the press before she died in 1965. 'We were like dragonflies,' she wrote in her autobiography, 'we seemed to be suspended effortlessly in the air, but in reality, our wings were beating very, very fast.'

ABOVE: studio portrait, 1926.
Photographer Ruth Harriet Louise

On screen Mary Pickford was 'Little Mary', 'The Girl with the Golden Curls', the helpless ragdoll Cinderella who never went to the ball. But off screen, this professional innocent took her career very much into her own hands. By 1916 it was said that 'whoever emerged in possession of a contract with Mary Pickford was going to hold the whip hand in the whole industry'. Her great achievement was to square the shrewd business woman with her screen persona as a guileless waif in movies such as *Tess of the Storm Country*, 1914, *Cinderella*, 1915, *The Foundling*, 1916, *Poor Little Rich Girl*, 1917, and *Daddy Long Legs*, 1919. She was all of twenty-seven and a multi-millionairess when she played the twelve-year-old orphan *Pollyanna* in 1920, one year after she joined forces with D. W. Griffith, Charlie Chaplin and Douglas Fairbanks Sr to form United Artists. Pickford married her charming Prince Fairbanks, and for a few frenzied years the two inspired adulation from all round the world. Their home, 'Pickfair', became a fairy-tale palace for Hollywood's favourite king and queen.

Pickford's famous golden curls surrounded a face which could look as hard as nails and just as unyielding. She never allowed her pull on an audience's emotions to waver for an instant; audiences returned the compliment by refusing to desert her for over twenty years. Her favoured cameraman Charles Rosher devised lighting techniques which helped her keep as fresh as apple-blossom as she slipped into her thirties. She did play mature roles; but in 1933, with fans clamouring for her to play Heidi, Alice in Wonderland or Cinderella again, she retired. 'I am sick of Cinderella parts, of wearing rags and tatters,' she admitted. 'I want to wear smart clothes and play the lover.'

ABOVE: studio portrait, c. 1918.
    Photographer Nelson Evans
RIGHT: *The Taming of the Shrew*, 1929, with
    Douglas Fairbanks Sr

COLLEEN MOORE

By the time she was twenty-five, Colleen Moore was earning a weekly salary of $12,500, a reflection of her value to a studio for whom she was a highly profitable jazz baby. With her bobbed hair, cheeky face and alert eyes, she resembles to modern eyes an uncanny combination of the better remembered Clara Bow and Louise Brooks. But in the 1920s, it was Moore who was *the* incarnation of the twenties flapper girl.

She had started as a dramatic actress in *Bad Boy* and *An Old-Fashioned Young Man*, 1917, cast as a return favour to her uncle for help over a censorship problem (her uncle was a famous Chicago newspaper editor, later fictionalized in 'The Front Page'). But after starring in Westerns opposite Tom Mix, in the title role of *Little Orphan Annie*, 1919, and opposite John Barrymore in *The Lotus Eater*, 1921, she struck it big in *Flaming Youth*, 1923. She built upon the flapper image with success and to great financial reward in *The Perfect Flapper* and *Flirting With Love*, both 1924, *We Moderns*, 1925, and *Synthetic Sin*, 1929. But she still tried for dramatic credibility with roles in *So Big*, 1925, *Irene*, 1926, and *Lilac Time*, 1928, with Gary Cooper, although to less popular acclaim. Her most remembered role is, however, not from the silent era, but in *The Power and the Glory*, 1933, opposite Spencer Tracy; her last talking film was a remake of *The Scarlet Letter*, 1934. After that she retired to enjoy her investments in the stock market. Her place in history will be assured not so much by her film performances as by a melancholic comment from author F. Scott Fitzgerald: 'I was the spark which lit up flaming youth. Colleen Moore was the torch. What little things we are to have caused such trouble.'

LEFT: studio portrait, c. 1928.
Photographer Elmer Fryer

When Louise Brooks was working as a shopgirl in Macy's in her mid-forties she was almost forgotten. Hollywood had shunned her, her movies were no longer shown, her name was a dim footnote in the film histories. But as other stars dimmed, her reputation grew. 'There is no Garbo', exclaimed Henri Langlois in the 1950s, 'only Louise Brooks.' To look at her early photos, all bobbed hair and flapper costumes, she seems a typical jazz baby of the 1920s. But not only did she possess an incandescent beauty and smile which appealed to both men and women, she also projected a peculiarly bewitching, pleasure-seeking aura.

At a time when many screen actresses were still hidebound by stilted stage techniques, Brooks incarnated a personality which was lively, magnetic and directly erotic. She had started out as a Ziegfeld showgirl, before getting roles in run of the mill pictures like *Just Another Blonde*, 1926, and *Rolled Stockings*, 1927, for Paramount. The next year she shone in a better part in Howard Hawks' *A Girl in Every Port*, and opposite Richard Arlen in Wellman's *Beggars of Life*, 1928, in which she brought a recognizably modern, androgynous quality to her role as a woman dressed as a man on the run on the freight trains. The German film director G.W. Pabst was so impressed by this twenty-three-year-old Kansas girl that he offered her the leading role as Lulu in an adaptation of Wedekind's plays, and Brooks packed her bags for Berlin. The change of scene worked wonders: 'I would be treated by Pabst with a kind of decency and respect unknown to me in Hollywood,' she later wrote. In *Die Büchse der Pandora/Pandora's Box*, 1929, she played a *femme fatale* living in a world of sexual pleasure. Brooks created a heroine who was intensely alive and tragic, an innocent who is yet a flirtatiously provocative symbol of amoral hedonism that fits exactly with our

RIGHT: studio portrait, c. 1928.
Photographer Eugene Robert Richee

modern interpretation of those times. Despite her two European successes – *Das Tagebuch einer Verlorenen/ Diary of a Lost Girl*, also directed by Pabst, was released in the same year as *Pandora's Box* – Brooks returned to Hollywood. But she was unwilling to bow down to dictates which she considered banal. She resisted unsuitable parts (such as the Harlow role in *The Public Enemy*), but was gradually crushed: in punishment for her disobedience, she was forced into accepting ever smaller roles. She scathingly described that dispiriting period of her career in a series of essays which she published from the fifties, long after she had abandoned her acting career and started to develop her capacity for articulate and penetrating film criticism.

Unsubdued by the Hollywood system, but ultimately defeated by it, Brooks, like Garbo, possessed a defiant pride and rebellious strength that has increased her standing over the years, the more so as general cynicism about the reality of 'Hollywood' has grown. Perhaps she herself came closest to defining her peculiar cinematic power when she wrote: 'The art of films does not consist of descriptive movement of face and body, but in the movements of thought and soul, transmitted in a kind of intense isolation.'

OPPOSITE: studio portrait, 1928.
    Photographer Eugene Robert Richee
ABOVE: publicity portrait for *The Canary Murder Case*, 1929
LEFT: publicity portrait for *Beggars of Life*, 1928, with Richard Arlen.
    Photographer Otto Dyar

CLARA BOW

Clara Bow was the 'It' girl: a rinky-dink little hotsy with sparkling eyes and a thoroughly modern hair-do, who was billed as 'The Hottest Baby of the Jazz Age'. She started her working life in Brooklyn as a telephone receptionist, but in 1922 at the age of sixteen won a beauty contest which took her to Hollywood. Her prize was a lot of hard work: forty-nine films in eight years.

Bow personified the era's pepped-up infatuation with living for kicks, and in *Daughters of Pleasure*, 1924, *The Plastic Age*, 1925, and *Fascinating Youth*, 1926, she resembled a fluttering moth endlessly drawn to a male light. In *It*, 1927, as a lingerie salesgirl who makes a beeline for her boss, she

personified the era's idea of sex appeal; batting her eyelids and flirtatiously glancing back over her shoulder, she became the heroine of America's new class of shopgirls in the big cities. With her flaming red hair, matching limousine and pet dogs, Bow played up to her reputation as a highly-sexed, fun-loving gal, and movies such as *Red Hair, Ladies of the Mob, The Fleet's In, Three Week-Ends*, all 1928, and *The Wild Party, Dangerous Curves* and *The Saturday Night Kid*, all 1929, suitably completed the picture.

But Bow's star waned towards the end of the decade. Her honking Brooklyn accent was, on the face of it, no asset when the talkies arrived, but she

might yet have survived had not her private life turned sour with a divorce scandal and stories of bad gambling debts. Then in 1930 her secretary revealed to a magazine the secrets of Bow's wild weekends with liquor, drugs and what seemed to be football teams of male admirers. The nervous strain soon showed in a breakdown. After her final film, *Hoopla*, 1933, for Fox, she retired with her husband to Nevada: the 'It' girl had just had enough. The girl they called 'Flaming Youth Personified' had burned out.

ABOVE: *The Wild Party*, 1929, with Fredric March
OPPOSITE: studio portrait, 1926.
Photographer Eugene Robert Richee

MARION DAVIES

In Orson Welles' epic film *Citizen Kane*, 1941, the career of Marion Davies was ultimately to make a greater movie than any in which she had starred. She had been a nineteen-year-old showgirl in 1916's 'Ziegfeld Follies' when she met a man who was to change her life: William Randolph Hearst, newspaper magnate and real-life model for Welles' Charles Foster Kane. Davies and Hearst fell genuinely in love but Hearst's wife would not give him a divorce. Instead he vowed to make Davies 'the greatest star in the nation'. Twenty years and $7 million later, even Hearst admitted failure.

In comedies such as *The Fair Co-Ed*, 1927, King Vidor's *The Patsy* and *Show People*, both 1928, Davies found her talent, satirizing flapper girl roles and even Swanson's regal style. But it was by then too late to establish herself as a light comedienne, thanks to Hearst's romantic penchant for her in more serious roles, such as the lead in the expensive flop *When Knighthood Was In Flower*, 1922. Despite Hearst's private agreements with the heads of Paramount and MGM, and his instructions that Miss Davies was to be mentioned at least once in each edition of his many newspapers, box office receipts for Davies' movies proclaimed their lack of popularity.

Eventually in 1934 her stay at MGM ended in acrimony after rivalry with Norma Shearer and her husband Irving Thalberg, vice-president of MGM. Davies had badly wanted the role of Elizabeth in *The Barretts of Wimpole Street*, and the lead role as *Marie Antoinette*: both went to Shearer. It was probably just as well. Davies had an awkward stammer (one of the few weaknesses not satirized by Welles), and her speeches in talkies had to be carefully limited. After four films at Warners, in 1937 Davies abandoned the attempt to become a star, but lived happily and richly ever after.

LEFT: studio portrait, 1928.
Photographer Apeda

When the Paris-made *Madame Sans-Gêne*, 1925, received its New York première in Times Square, Gloria Swanson arrived with a real-life Marquis as her (third) husband to be treated like royalty. Her name was given the largest billing ever seen, spelt out in electric lights along the entire façade of the cinema, with the American flag and French tricolour flapping in the wind. 'I have decided that when I am a star, I will be every inch and every moment the star,' she once said.

Swanson's father was Swedish-Italian, her mother of Polish-French-German stock, and Swanson's looks were thought to combine both waif and vamp-like qualities. After a spell as a 'Sennett Girl', she found her svengali in the young Cecil B. DeMille at Paramount for a series of bold, scandalous, sex-laced movies such as *Male and Female, Don't Change Your Husband*, both 1919, and *Why Change Your Wife?*, 1920. Swanson brought middle America into shocked contact with the roaring twenties. Without inhibition she indulged America's fascination for adultery, luxury, love triangles and female sexual discovery. Swanson mocked the movies' self-imposed moralizing. She glorified in the trappings of sexual fetishes, the satin lingerie, the jewelled headdresses, silk gowns, chiffon hats and expensive furs; and sported a narrow-lipped expression and tight hairstyle that seemed almost matronly.

Swanson was always a gift for Paramount's publicists, who, among other schemes, cooked up a feud between her and rival Pola Negri. But in 1926 she turned down offers of $17,500 a week to make her own movies through United Artists. A dispute between herself and director Erich von Stroheim wrecked their perversely brilliant *Queen Kelly*, 1928, although she recovered from disaster by winning an Oscar nomination for her part as *Sadie Thompson*, 1928.

Swanson made more pictures, but

RIGHT: studio portrait, 1919.
　　Photographer Nelson Evans

her ascendancy waned with the Depression years, when her wild extravagance and regal persona appeared almost embarrassing. It never stopped her returning in style. When she played the silent star Norma Desmond in Billy Wilder's *Sunset Boulevard*, 1950, she was still only fifty-three, but her era seemed centuries away. 'I am still big,' she says in character. 'It's the pictures that got smaller.' That sad mixture of overblown pride and undeniable truth will remain her epitaph.

RIGHT: studio publicity, c. 1920
BELOW: *Queen Kelly*, 1928, with Walter Byron
OPPOSITE: studio portrait, 1941.
        Photographer Ernest A. Bachrach

THE CLASSICS

The end of the 1920s brought a wind of change which was irreversible, strong, and, for many, bitterly cold. The arrival of the Talkies in 1927, the Stock Market Crash of 1929, and the Depression of the 1930s swept away many of the silent stars like unwanted old leaves. For some, attitudes just went out of fashion. The extravagances of Gloria Swanson suddenly seemed decadent, as if caught in a time warp; Clara Bow's 'It' girl burned out doing the Charleston; Marion Davies was revealed to have a nervous stutter; Pola Negri returned to Germany; Mary Pickford finally hung up her Pollyanna pigtails, divorced Fairbanks, 'retired' to Pickfair, and took to drink. Others, like Vilma Banky and Norma Talmadge, just drifted away; Mae Murray mishandled her contract negotiations, and even Lillian Gish experienced the chill of public resentment and studio indifference, branded a 'sexless antique'. Along with their leading men like John Gilbert, Ramon Novarro and Douglas Fairbanks Sr, these goddesses discovered that their immortal reign was liable to come to a brusque and often cruel end.

Those who passed the test of microphone audibility and audience capriciousness seemed also to increase their fame. Survivors like Garbo, Crawford and Shearer ascended to legendary heights. Along with Myrna Loy, Judy Garland and Greer Garson, they were to form the brightest constellation in MGM's galaxy of stars, exemplifying that studio's reputation for elegance, sophistication and style. With Jeanette MacDonald and Nelson Eddy warbling their light operettas, and a host of leading men that included Clark Gable, Spencer Tracy, Robert Taylor and William Powell, MGM entertained Depression America and the world with sumptuous escapist fantasies, designed and groomed to perfection by art director Cedric Gibbons and costume designer Adrian, all under Irving Thalberg's creative control.

Warner Brothers, the studio whose profits had swollen after their espousal of sound, aimed for the opposite in their house style. With leading men like James Cagney, Paul Muni, and Edward G. Robinson they rode high on a gangster cycle that took its stories from the newspaper headlines and its hard-boiled style from the tough-guy atmosphere of cities like New York and Chicago. Humphrey Bogart and Errol Flynn would later join Olivia De Havilland in spectacular action adventures, but Bette Davis just got on with perfecting her persona in tough-hearted little melodramas so tightly budgeted they even made her cry. Meanwhile, Busby Berkeley glorified lines of chorus girls into living hymns to the machine age, creating an abstract world of surreal eroticism.

Other studios had less well defined, but nevertheless distinct, styles. Paramount became famous for its strong European influences of wit and sophistication, with leading directors like Ernst Lubitsch, Rouben Mamoulian, and Josef von Sternberg directing Marlene Dietrich. Soon Claudette Colbert, Sylvia Sidney, Kay Francis and Fredric March joined the studio from the theatre as open call went out for actors and actresses who could speak dialogue. Gary Cooper and George Raft were later joined by Fred MacMurray, Bing Crosby, Bob Hope and, of course, Dorothy Lamour, while the studio's reputation for comedy thrived with Mae West, W.C. Fields and the Marx Brothers snatched from vaudeville and the stage. A new organization, RKO, boasted Katharine Hepburn in drama and the leading musical team of Ginger Rogers and Fred Astaire, while Universal specialized in a horror cycle of *Frankenstein* and *Dracula* with Boris Karloff and Bela Lugosi, and later branched out into a spate of Deanna Durbin musicals. Columbia benefited from Frank Capra's comic expertise, and Fox kept afloat on The Good Ship Lollipop with Shirley Temple, before attracting Alice Faye, Tyrone Power and Don Ameche to their roster.

Despite the often punitive conditions attached to stars' seven-year contracts, and the niggling petty discipline demanded by autocrats like Jack Warner or Columbia's Harry Cohn, the rewards were great and in general actors and actresses never had it so good. The sheer quantity of movies rolling off the studio production lines into distribution around the world would have ensured lasting fame for the leading ladies of the 1930s. Of course, overwork caused untold pressures, and bad scripts came to the top of the pile too often, demanding typecast performances from jaded stars. But even if stars like Bette Davis chafed, and if others like Garbo, Dietrich and Crawford found themselves eased out of their top niches by the end of the decade by wily studio bosses, they had reaped the benefits of an immensely productive system.

As to the stars themselves, Garbo dominated them all by her sheer charismatic elegance, deftly steering herself through roles which created an insurmountable image of aristocratic beauty and disdain. Compared to her, Norma Shearer was a cardboard mediocrity, while Bette Davis, Joan Crawford and Barbara Stanwyck wallowed in melodrama, and Dietrich became immobilized by a glamorous eroticism that bordered on parody. These actresses made good use of their silent heritage, drawing on lessons already learnt by them or their predecessors; but sound in all its novelty was producing a new breed. Machine-gun-style dialogue or wisecracking fast talking from the mouths of Ginger Rogers, Rosalind Russell, Joan Blondell, Carole Lombard or Jean Harlow brought these stars closer to the human scale of things. Mae West's voice ebbed and flowed through her single-*entendres* with practised ease, while Harlow's guttersnipe snarl punched venom and spite into the most innocuous dialogue. Their unashamed eroticism within the respective confines of an 1890s gown or a low-cut silk dress brought censors rushing for their blue pencils, and a new moral code kept this good-humouredly playful sexuality in check from the mid-1930s. Independent ladies like Katharine Hepburn, Carole Lombard, Rosalind Russell or Ginger Rogers outraged and outwitted the world in which dwelt tame males like Cary Grant, Melvyn Douglas and Fred MacMurray. Myrna Loy, meanwhile, kept house for William Powell in the *Thin Man* series of comedies, which for the first time treated marriage realistically but romantically, as something more than a shouting match and something less than heavenly choirs.

Despite the language barriers brought by sound, the American film industry's economic vibrancy ensured its worldwide domination. While Germany's cinema continued in uncertain taste under the Nazis, France's films reflected a low-key poeticism which rarely competed with Yankee glamour, and the British offered home-grown musicals and Korda's historical epics as contributions to the international market. Hollywood was indisputably the world centre for escapist entertainment on the movie screen, with its boundless optimism countering real-life Depression and international political events. The earlier efforts during the silent era to find plots, players, settings and emotions which could transcend the country's own vast differences of language, background and traditions now came into good use. Typecasting – the refinement of immediately recognizable characters and the careful identification of these with specific actresses – was something at which Hollywood truly excelled. Just as early immigrants had understood the countless variations on the themes of the Cinderella story or The Kiss, now audiences all over the world could recognize a Garbo, Harlow, Bette Davis or Claudette Colbert – and anticipate what she would do.

Failure to conform totally to these high standards, however, brought a ruthless penalty. These classic leading ladies represented a dream machine producing fantasies at full tilt. Their instincts, talents, smiles, laughs and frowns were imprinted upon the memories of the world by an industry which regarded them as prize commodities and paid them accordingly: in 1935 Marlene Dietrich earned $368,000, Madeleine Carroll $350,000, and Mae West became the highest-paid woman in the USA with a salary of $480,000. But unlike most leading men, few were to survive past their late thirties as such highly-prized attractions. A slight slip in box office popularity could mean a drastic cut in salary, and unless executive protection was provided, even exclusion from leading roles altogether. Replacements for these classics were continually sought, who might be younger, weaker, cheaper and more pliable – as if the Garbos, Dietrichs, Harlows and Hepburns were merely moulds from which replicas could be fashioned. The decade ended with the epic hunt for a Scarlett O'Hara for *Gone With the Wind*, Hollywood's role of a lifetime. The prime part of a Southern belle caused everyone from Norma Shearer to Joan Crawford to petition for consideration. In the end it went to a young English actress, Vivien Leigh; she was understandably highly pleased, highly resented, and paid all of $15,000.

GRETA GARBO

Garbo was not always considered the unique and irreplaceable star she seems today. In the mid-1920s, when she was first brought to Hollywood by MGM as the protégé of Swedish director Mauritz Stiller, she was considered an exotic leading lady in the neurotically sensitive tradition of Gloria Swanson or Pola Negri. But in contrast to their overwrought artifice, Garbo brought something new from her Swedish background: simplicity, realism and sincerity. Alone among her contemporaries, she intuitively grasped that the great thrill of cinema was to share a moment of private

OPPOSITE: studio portrait, 1931.
         Photographer Clarence Sinclair Bull
LEFT: *Love*, 1927, with John Gilbert
BELOW: *The Single Standard*, 1929, with
         Nils Asther

revelation with an audience, and this at a time in movie history when, in the words of Roland Barthes, 'capturing the human face still plunged audiences into the deepest ecstasy'.

Garbo was born Greta Louisa Gustafsson, the daughter of a Stockholm labourer. At sixteen she was already playing bit-parts in movies, and by twenty she had attracted the attention of Stiller. He changed her name and put her into *Gösta Berlings Saga*, 1924, which won critical acclaim in Europe. It was only by virtue of Stiller's new contract with MGM, which had as one of its conditions that Garbo should also be put on the payroll, that this diffident star arrived in Hollywood. The reluctant studio had little idea of how to use her. They tried all the usual publicity gambits — posing her with animals, in swimsuits, or even as a healthy athlete testing her biceps — without success. Fortunately her early rebellion against this crude pigeonholing coincided with rapturous acclaim for her American debut in *The Torrent*, 1926. Her insistent reticence was turned to advantage by MGM, who promoted her as a reclusive mystery. Thus was born one of this century's great legends.

She resembled an ethereal vamp in her forcefully erotic silent movies with John Gilbert — *Love* and *Flesh and the Devil*, both 1927, and *A Woman of Affairs*, 1929. If her attitude to love in these films seems blasé, her appreciation of its responsibilities is profound. She is at once fickle and severe, projecting such contradictions with tragic appeal. From the moment when she uttered her first line of dialogue in *Anna Christie*, 1930, she became MGM's leading light: more noble than Shearer, more classy than Harlow, more discreet than Crawford.

Garbo's first classic role was as *Queen Christina*, 1933. In that film her face resembles a mask of alabaster, a blank page upon which audiences

OPPOSITE: publicity portrait for *Romance*, 1930.
Photographer George Hurrell
ABOVE: *Mata Hari*, 1931, with Ramon Novarro
LEFT: *Grand Hotel*, 1932, with John Barrymore

could inscribe all manner of emotion and heartbreak. This was subtle and intelligent direction by Rouben Mamoulian, in a style Garbo was to make her own. With title roles as *Anna Karenina*, 1935, and *Camille*, 1936, she perfected the role of the distraught lover. Another elaborate costume drama, *Conquest*, 1937, developed that persona, as Maria Walewska to Charles Boyer's Napoleon, but by now her popularity was greater outside the USA. *Ninotchka*, 1939, advertised as the movie in which 'Garbo laughs', allowed her a change of image, but MGM remained unsympathetic to a star who had always refused to toe the line, and after *Two-Faced Woman*, 1941, Garbo went into a temporary retirement that became permanent.

Her disappearance from the screen paradoxically increased her stature, and made real the hyperbole of MGM publicity. She had brought cinema itself to maturity by yoking the silents' sense of gesture and drama to the realism of the talkies, but remained an enigmatic and unreachable phenomenon. Just look at Garbo's face. Sometimes her strong bones and arched eyebrows are only just visible; the eyes are shaded beneath long lashes that cast shadows on her skin; her hair crowns her forehead and her lips are concealed as if they hold secrets waiting to be revealed. She seems to wish she were invisible: it is not so much a face as a shadow of one, suggested by isolated glimpses and memories, inscrutable and austere. In such a style, she exercised dominion over the earliest secrets of cinema.

LEFT: *Camille*, 1936, with Robert Taylor
OPPOSITE: publicity portrait for *Queen Christina*, 1933.
Photographer Clarence Sinclair Bull

NORMA SHEARER

Sleek and sophisticated, poised and elegant, Norma Shearer diligently fulfilled her role as MGM's 'first lady of the screen' in the early thirties. As the mink-clad heroine of *The Divorcee*, 1930, or the regal wife of MGM's vice-president Irving Thalberg, she was never less than a class act beloved by the public and envied by her rivals: 'How can I compete with Norma', Joan Crawford is supposed to have pondered, 'when she sleeps with the boss?'

It is indeed hard to imagine Shearer as a carefree young flapper, climbing the show business ladder in the early 1920s. From Miss Lotta Miles in tyre advertisements she climbed to frothy movies like *Pleasure Mad*, 1923, and from there the ladder led upwards to leading roles in such films as *Let Us Be Gay*, 1930, and to an Academy Award for her portrayal of the young married in *The Divorcee*. By then her specialization was for what Pauline Kael once called 'sexy suffering in satin gowns', often at the hands of Robert Montgomery. She projected a slightly careful and sensible attitude towards passion's wilder moments, which was quite the reverse of MGM's Harlow or Garbo. Elevated to the virginal purity of Elizabeth Barrett in *The Barretts of Wimpole Street*, 1934, and to a memorably aged, thirty-five-year-old Juliet in *Romeo and Juliet*, 1936, Shearer seemed a lady from a more moral century, nobly contemplating the foibles of mortals as a real-life *Marie Antoinette*, 1938. Surrounded by such go-getters as Joan Crawford and Rosalind Russell in *The Women*, 1939, she seemed desperately conventional, and her decisions to reject the leading roles in *Gone With the Wind* and *Mrs Miniver* were probably wise.

OPPOSITE: studio portrait, 1931.
    Photographer George Hurrell
ABOVE: publicity portrait for *Marie Antoinette*, 1938.
    Photographer Laszlo Willinger
LEFT: *A Free Soul*, 1931, with Clark Gable

FAY WRAY

JANET GAYNOR

Blond hair streaming in the wind, torn dress revealing her supine body, Fay Wray is most memorable as the unwilling inamorata of the giant ape *King Kong*, 1933. In dramatic terms her role as Ann Darrow may have offered little more than a test of lung power; but as an object of passion in a nightmarish fantasy of seduction, she has become a potent icon. Following a part in Erich von Stroheim's *The Wedding March*, 1928, she had been given lead roles opposite such stars as Gary Cooper and Fredric March. But it was as a 'scream queen' ravaged by demented scientists and moon monsters in movies like *Doctor X*, 1932, that she really found fame. She brought a novelty to her roles that goes beyond her camp popularity.

BELOW: publicity portrait for *King Kong*, 1933.
Photographer Robert W. Coburn

Dimpled and coy as the sweet, abandoned young wife in Murnau's *Sunrise*, 1927, Janet Gaynor proved so poignant that her performance, along with those in *Seventh Heaven*, also 1927, and *Street Angel*, 1928, won her the first Oscar as Best Actress. Her waif-like innocence was often cast opposite Charles Farrell, and by the early thirties the pair had become 'America's favourite lovebirds'. She graduated to more mature roles, such as in the original *A Star is Born*, 1937. Despite her little-girl-lost looks, Gaynor proved neither winsome nor saccharine. Instead she possessed a tragic quality of reserve and suppressed emotion that could galvanize a simple tale into a whirl of tears and heart-rending melodrama.

ABOVE: *A Star is Born*, 1937

Filed under Mexican/Exotic, Dolores Del Rio certainly possessed a hotter aura than did all the scrawny WASP hopefuls flooding Hollywood in the thirties. Her south-of-the-border beauty suggested wild and wonderful passions to both audiences and producers, and caused David O. Selznick to deliver the immortal lines, 'I want Del Rio and [Joel] McCrea in a South Seas romance . . . I don't care what story you use so long as we call it *Bird of Paradise* and Del Rio jumps into a flaming volcano at the finish.' They travelled off to the South Seas with director King Vidor and did just that.

Del Rio had first attracted the attention of director Edwin Carewe at the age of twenty in Mexico. She came to Hollywood and soon began to get leading roles opposite Victor McLaglen in *What Price Glory?*, 1926, *The Loves of Carmen* and *Resurrection*, both 1927, and *Ramona*, 1928, which at last brought her stardom. Del Rio specialized in the vampish gypsy or peasant girl, but quickly became typecast. In a series of early thirties movies, *The Bad One*, 1930, *Bird of Paradise*, 1932, *Flying Down to Rio*, 1933, and *Madame Du Barry*, 1934, she gradually came to resemble a beautiful species of exotic plant shifted about in front of a variety of backdrops: remarkable, but somehow lacking in drama. Ironically, the period coincided with her marriage to Cedric Gibbons, the famous MGM art director. Her well-publicized romance with Orson Welles bore fruit in *Journey Into Fear* in 1942, but despite her ambitions, Hollywood only required her to fit a label. So a year later she returned to Mexico, where a lucrative contract gave her a percentage of the profits from her films; on screen and stage her Mexican career proved both more successful and more intellectually rewarding. In the sixties she drifted back to Hollywood from time to time, taking character roles in movies like *Cheyenne Autumn*, 1964.

RIGHT: *In Caliente*, 1935, with Phil Regan

TALLULAH BANKHEAD

'Hello, daaahling!' The distinctly husky greeting of Southern belle Tallulah Bankhead made history, despite a less than satisfying movie career. With her bitchy witticisms and self-mocking tone, she tended to be more interesting – and more successful – off than on the screen. Tennessee Williams wrote 'A Streetcar Named Desire' with Bankhead in mind as Blanche Dubois; and Bette Davis' loud-mouthed Margo Channing in *All About Eve*, 1950, bore more than a superficial likeness to her (which Bankhead didn't fail to notice).

Tallulah (and that was her real name) was the daughter of a wealthy Alabama politician who later became Speaker of the House of Representa-tives. When the teenage Tallulah won a beauty contest, she was introduced to the New York stage; and in her early twenties, after a couple of screen roles, she moved to London where she became a celebrated stage success. In 1928, towards the end of her eight-year stay, Bankhead made *His House in Order* and *A Woman's Law*, and on her arrival in Hollywood found studio executives fighting for her. Paramount won, but having done so seemed at a loss to know what to do with her. She was pushed as a reserve-team Dietrich in an early Cukor movie, *Tarnished Lady*, 1931, and she dutifully went through the motions in *My Sin*, 1931, with Fredric March, and *Devil and the Deep*, 1932, with a choice of Charles Laughton, Cary Grant and Gary Cooper. But after leading with Robert Montgomery in *Faithless*, 1932, she gave up movies to concentrate on an already triumphant stage career.

Bankhead was to have her revenge on Hollywood with an award for her performance in Hitchcock's *Lifeboat*, 1944, where she rules the roost on a tiny craft bobbing on the ocean. Always larger than life, in Hollywood her reward proved to be roles too thin for her talents.

ABOVE: publicity portrait for *Thunder Below*, 1932.
Photographer Irving Lippman

In *Shanghai Express*, 1932, Dietrich and Anna May Wong walk down the platform, exciting the gaze of awe-struck males who might yet become their victims . . . . Predatory, beguiling, a mysterious oriental temptress designed and decorated to studio specifications, Wong survived obviously typecast roles by her stunning screen presence. Born in Los Angeles' China-town, she graduated at the age of sixteen to the role of Arabian slavegirl opposite Douglas Fairbanks Sr in *The Thief of Bagdad*, 1924. Clad in satin bikini and bizarre headdress, and draped in beads, she was difficult to ignore. Throughout the twenties a vogue for oriental beauty guaranteed her steady work in US, German and British film productions, from *Streets of Shanghai* and *The Chinese Parrot*, both 1927, to *Wasted Love*, 1928, and *Piccadilly*, 1929. Bejewelled and encased in high-collared gowns, the name of Anna May Wong became synonymous with the inscrutable, un-knowable Orient. She was a principal inhabitant of a Shanghai-Baghdad of the Californian imagination that sought to combine the perfection of a Ming vase with the availability of a Shanghai whore. Her career spanned the thirties, but the movies got worse and worse: her parts ranged from gang-ster's moll to mysterious villainess in cheap melodramas and detective movies. Highlights included *Lime-house Blues*, 1934, opposite George Raft, Robert Florey's *Daughter of Shanghai* three years later, and *Dangerous to Know*, 1938. She retired from the movies in 1942, aged only thirty-five, but did return to appear in the odd film before her death in 1961.

RIGHT: studio portrait, 1934.
    Photographer Ray Jones

MAE WEST

Dressed like an inflatable Venus in feathers and pearls, Mae West combined the wit of Oscar Wilde, the roguery of W.C. Fields, and the allure of a bar-room Salome in a style which meant only one thing to most audiences: 'Sex'. That was the title of the 1926 revue that West wrote, directed and produced, and which earned her a jail sentence for obscenity. The daughter of a boxer, West made her first appearance on the stage aged five, and became 'The Baby Vamp'. Movies didn't discover her until she was forty, when she made her film and screenwriting debut with *Night After Night*, 1932. She was as good a reason as any for inventing the talkies, and with *She Done Him Wrong* and *I'm No Angel*, both 1933 and with Cary Grant, and with *Belle of the Nineties*, 1934, she set up a run of hits which made her one of the richest women in America. She revolutionized public acceptance of sexual matters with a constant stream of witty dialogue, innuendo and single-*entendres*, most of which she wrote herself. Despite a backlash from censors in the mid-thirties, she persevered in *Go West Young Man*, 1936, *Every Day's a Holiday*, 1937, and with her peer W. C. Fields in *My Little Chickadee*, 1940; but as the decade ended she returned to Broadway and the international nightclub circuit as a legend in her own lifetime. The disaster of *Myra Breckinridge*, 1970, could not diminish her popularity, nor could her appearance as an eighty-five-year-old vamp in the lamentable *Sextette*, 1978. When she died in 1980 she was mourned by more than the drag queens who had borrowed her style. Immortal lines like 'Come up and see me sometime', and 'Peel me a grape' are still quoted in affectionate parody more than half a century after she first spoke them; not many scriptwriters can boast as much.

LEFT: publicity portrait for *I'm No Angel*, 1933.
Photographer Don English
OPPOSITE: studio portrait, 1938.
Photographer Eugene Robert Richee

MIRIAM HOPKINS

MARY ASTOR

A public scandal played a curiously positive part in Mary Astor's career. She had been a silent lead opposite Douglas Fairbanks Sr and John Barrymore, and in *Red Dust*, 1932, she had gamely competed with Jean Harlow in MGM's jungle swamps for Clark Gable's affections. Her career flagged. Then, when divorcing her second husband, her private diaries disclosing lurid details of her affairs became public. She never looked back. She played her best roles in *Dodsworth*, 1936, in *Woman Against Woman*, 1938, as an acid-tongued bitch, and in a Bette Davis movie, *The Great Lie*, 1941. She was even better opposite Humphrey Bogart in *The Maltese Falcon* 1941, where her deception and cunning ensured her classic status.

BELOW: studio portrait, 1940.
Photographer A. L. 'Whitey' Schaefer

Miriam Hopkins had all the impact of a star, even if she lacked acting ability to match. She featured strongly in *Trouble in Paradise*, 1932, and opposite Fredric March and Gary Cooper in *Design for Living*, 1933. Two years later she shone as the scheming heroine in Mamoulian's screen version of Thackeray's 'Vanity Fair', *Becky Sharp*. The role lent itself to her strengths and she played it to the hilt; but the film's technical novelty – as the first feature to use three-strip Technicolor – detracted from her moment of glory. Hopkins continued to star with the likes of Edward G. Robinson, Joel McCrea, Paul Muni and Bette Davis, but by the early forties her movie career had faltered and she returned to the Broadway stage.

ABOVE: studio portrait, 1934.
Photographer Eugene Robert Richee

MADELEINE CARROLL

In the Hollywood atlas of the world all Swedish women were brooding, all French passionate, all Mexicans spitfires, and all the English were refined, reticent, or aloof, possessing naturally a certain touch of class. Madeleine Carroll was an early English export to Hollywood who did not disappoint these expectations.

Yet it took a British director like Alfred Hitchcock to exploit the appeal of the English and perversely turn it into humiliation. Handcuffed to suspected murderer Robert Donat in the British-made *The 39 Steps*, 1935, Carroll is in turn stern, impudent, coquettish and outraged. Although her role is lightly comic, she steers it into a visible prototype for Hitchcock's later ice blondes. Carroll did even better in his *The Secret Agent*, 1936, with John Gielgud and Peter Lorre; and by the time she departed for Hollywood later that year her limpid looks were being described as among the most beautiful in the world. Once at 20th Century Fox on a contract to Walter Wanger, she effortlessly rose to prominence opposite Ronald Colman in *The Prisoner of Zenda*, 1937. She was an ideal partner, her face resembling a blank page, a mask on which all Colman's swashbuckling desires could be projected. In a series of movies teamed with Fred MacMurray, Tyrone Power or husband Sterling Hayden (she married four times in all), she managed to be all things to all men, a popular romantic lead of remarkable elegance but one who lacked the inner drive that might have distinguished her as dramatically special.

Carroll became an American citizen in 1943, after returning from war work in Britain following the Blitz of London. She was to make only three films after the end of the war.

RIGHT: studio portrait, c. 1936.
Photographer William Walling Jr

JEAN HARLOW

One early photograph of the teenage Harlean Carpenter, a Kansas City dentist's daughter, shows her almost as a Pre-Raphaelite icon. Her fair hair tumbles over her brow, her peachy skin and natural beauty are suffused with an old-fashioned ethereal glow. Some five years later Harlean was photographed as a rising young Hollywood starlet. The difference is uncanny. Her hair, now dyed platinum blonde, is tight and wavy, scraped off her forehead to show arched pencilled eyebrows, mascara-ed eyes and skin like a mask. Her new look is direct,

OPPOSITE: studio portrait, 1932.
      Photographer George Hurrell
LEFT: studio portrait, c. 1931.
      Photographer Clarence Sinclair Bull
BELOW: *Red Dust*, 1932, with Clark Gable

brazen, delighting in cheap dime-store artifice. She looks as if she has just put her foot down and accelerated into the twentieth century – and that the century itself now belongs to Jean Harlow.

In Hollywood lore she is the first platinum blonde, a shooting star who burned herself out at the age of twenty-six after a life illuminated by photographers' flashbulbs. After Monroe's death she was resurrected in a brief but trashy cult, and her roles as an MGM goddess, gum-chewing tramp, leading lady to Clark Gable, Cagney and William Powell, or just as the gossip columnists' favourite, have all become blurred. Photographed like a silent movie star in white satin, but with her guttural Missouri accent endearing her to the first talkies' audiences, she was simply America's favourite talking blonde.

In MGM's *Red Dust*, 1932, she was

visibly in her ascendancy. 'Scrub my back!' she barks to a stunned Gable while she stands naked in a makeshift shower. She shocked and delighted audiences when she asked Jimmy Cagney for his telephone number in *The Public Enemy*, 1931, or bad-mouthed her gruesome spouse Wallace Beery in the otherwise elegant *Dinner at Eight*, 1933. Through those early crackling speakers in the movie theatres Harlow sounded great, and screenplays from the ranks of Anita Loos or Dorothy Parker played on that brittle, wisecracking style she was to make her own.

By the mid-1930s Harlow was un-assailable, regularly attracting over twenty million movie-goers. This was the girl who had started out as a film extra after eloping to Los Angeles aged sixteen, and who had caught the eye of Howard Hughes for *Hell's Angels*,

1930; this was the girl whose performances had been panned by the critics until she signed with MGM in 1932, and whose screen persona had now meshed with real life in *Bombshell*, 1933, *Platinum Blonde*, 1931, or *The Girl from Missouri*, 1934. Her best latter-day role, opposite William Powell in *Libeled Lady*, 1936, showed she was maturing as an actress just as her time was about to pass. She died of uremic poisoning after completing *Saratoga*, in 1937, and at her funeral fans ransacked the flowers for souvenirs. By then the platinum hair and the satin had all but obliterated the Pre-Raphaelite beauty of ten years before.

ABOVE: studio portrait, 1933.
Photographer Clarence Sinclair Bull
OPPOSITE: publicity portrait for *Bombshell*, 1933.
Photographer George Hurrell

KAY FRANCIS

SYLVIA SIDNEY

Sylvia Sidney was one of the few stars of the thirties who portrayed a working-class girl on her own (usually suffering) merits. She excelled as the trembling lover of born loser Henry Fonda in Fritz Lang's *You Only Live Once*, 1937, a downbeat outlaw story in which she achieves intense pathos without melodrama. She took other leading roles for Lang in *Fury*, 1936, and *You and Me*, 1938, and brought a wide-eyed innocence to such classics as Mamoulian's *City Streets*, 1931, and Hitchcock's *Sabotage*, 1936. She was continually irked by her typecasting in unhappy roles, but her long-suffering look and valiant heroism are the key to her immense appeal to cinema audiences everywhere throughout the Depression years.

BELOW: *You Only Live Once*, 1937, with Henry Fonda

A leading lady for Paramount and later Warner Bros., Kay Francis perfected a niche as the virtuous, suffering type. Her appeal has undeniably dated with the years, despite her strong performances in Lubitsch's *Trouble in Paradise* and King Vidor's *Cynara*, both 1932. She made a popular team with William Powell, but the plot of their smash hit *One Way Passage*, 1932, now sounds unbearably mawkish: she plays a girl with an incurable disease on an ocean voyage, who falls in love with Powell, a convicted criminal on his way to prison. By the late thirties her tear-stained performances had fallen so far in popularity that her annual salary of $227,500 — higher than that of Bette Davis at the time — and her crown at Warners could no longer be justified.

ABOVE: *Raffles*, 1930, with Ronald Colman

Jean Arthur was taking custard pies in the face and riding out on the vogue for B Westerns for years before she finally found her form. Once a dark-haired beauty, she turned blonde; the talkies brought her husky, cracked voice over the speakers; and her flair for light comedy made her a national favourite. The turning point was John Ford's *The Whole Town's Talking*, 1935, with Edward G. Robinson: Arthur played the tough-talking salesgirl with an answer for everything. Though she was good as Calamity Jane in *The Plainsman*, 1937, with Gary Cooper, and charmed Charles Boyer in *History is Made at Night*, 1937, she peaked as director Frank Capra's favourite actress. In three of his fables of Depression America she epitomized a brand of hard-boiled quirkiness that took in screwball events as the most natural things in the world. She played a reporter warming to country cousin Gary Cooper's eccentric ways in *Mr Deeds Goes to Town*, 1936; she co-starred with James Stewart in *You Can't Take It With You*, 1938, and the remarkable *Mr Smith Goes to Washington* 1939, parables of naïve common sense pitting its wits against big-business logic. Arthur was the perfect foil for Stewart, an amusing livewire next to his slow hick laziness; she rallies to his aid and wins the day, of course. She followed this with a gem of a part as the stranded showgirl in Howard Hawks' *Only Angels Have Wings*, 1939, in which she has a bad crush on boss Cary Grant. She received an Academy Award nomination in 1943 for a less interesting part in *The More the Merrier* with Joel McCrea, and director George Stevens piled praise on her as 'one of the greatest comediennes the world has ever seen'. But after years of quarrelling with Columbia's boss Harry Cohn, it is reported that she jumped for joy when her contract was terminated. She returned to the screen only twice.

RIGHT: studio portrait, 1937.
 Photographer Robert W. Coburn

CAROLE LOMBARD

When she died in a plane crash in 1942, aged only thirty-four, Carole Lombard was already a favourite with the American public and known as one of its finest comediennes. As Mrs Clark Gable, she was also one half of show business' most glamorous couple. She had spent the twenties playing in routine movies for more than one studio, but from the time she found her true form in *Twentieth Century*, 1934, Lombard became a prime example of how swiftly the studio system could exploit and promote a rising star and yet produce dynamic results.

In a favourite train compartment scene in *Twentieth Century*, Lombard shouts, yelps, stamps her feet, curses and storms against the wily John Barrymore, who plays an outrageously ham actor–manager. She is petite, wiry, glamorous; he is gargantuan, like a comic gargoyle. As she persists in defying him, the scene mounts to fever pitch, with Lombard controlling the ricocheting dialogue of Ben Hecht and Charles MacArthur in double-quick time. With this film she became a top-rank star, and set the standard for the screwball comedies of the next decade. For before this, such rebellious female behaviour would have been frowned upon, acceptable only in the topsy-turvy world of the anarchic Mack Sennett comedies in which Lombard had herself spent two years in 1927–8. Now she stamped an identity on her era, and turned that brand of disruptive, manic energy into a positive quality: 'wackiness'. In *My Man Godfrey*, 1936, *Nothing Sacred*, 1937, and her crowning glory *To Be Or Not To Be*, 1942, Lombard waged good-natured war against middle-class restraint, conventions and conformity.

In *My Man Godfrey*, Lombard is the spoiled little rich girl who chases after the new butler (William Powell – in real life her husband from 1931 to 1933). Her celebration of a woman's need to

LEFT: studio portrait, 1932.
Photographer Eugene Robert Richee

satisfy her desires is symptomatic of the new climate of female self-confidence, and only in such an atmosphere could Lombard have expressed such bemused bewilderment at the idea of *not* satisfying the pleasure principle. It was a performance that won her the only Oscar nomination of her career. In *Nothing Sacred* Lombard is the pivot around which a bitter satire turns. She plays a young girl who becomes headline news when it is found she is dying of radium poisoning. Such a gift for black comedy was rare in Hollywood stars, but Lombard's role

LEFT: off set *The Princess Comes Across*, 1936.
Photographer Don English
BELOW: publicity portrait for *The Gay Bride*, 1934,
with Chester Morris.
Photographer Clarence Sinclair Bull

in Ernst Lubitsch's satire, *To Be Or Not To Be*, showed her to be a master of it, ensnared in a farce of Warsaw actors impersonating wartime Nazis. It was her last film. But it underlined the fact that Lombard had brought Hollywood a new sophistication without losing the rough and ready, small-town attitudes upon which both she and the famous film capital thrived.

RIGHT: studio portrait, 1936.
   Photographer William Walling Jr
BELOW: studio publicity, c. 1937, with
   Clark Gable
OPPOSITE: studio portrait, 1941.
   Photographer Robert W. Coburn

MYRNA LOY

Myrna Loy made over sixty movies before 1932 in roles that ran the gamut of Hollywood exotic: a mysterious vamp, evil seductress, oriental torturer, South Seas temptress, or slavegirl clad in grass skirts. But for the next fifteen years she was to achieve fame as their polar opposite: as the wittily acerbic Nora Charles, who first appeared on screen with husband Nick – William Powell – in W. S. Van Dyke's *The Thin Man*, 1934.

Loy started out as a dancer at Grauman's Chinese Theater on Hollywood Boulevard, and patiently worked through dozens of production line movies before her flair for light comedy was recognized. In 1932 she signed with MGM, and in 1934 'Woody' Van Dyke noticed the peculiar

chemistry of Loy and Powell on screen together – they had just done *Manhattan Melodrama*, 1934, with Clark Gable – and cast the pair in his version of the Dashiell Hammett thriller, *The Thin Man*. It was a smash hit. Loy and Powell seemed to strike a chord with their crackling dialogue and seemingly effortless verbal fencing. Loy's portrayal of Nora was immensely influential at a time when other screen wives were invariably cast as frumpy nags or glamorous gold diggers. She was suave and sophisticated, more often seen wielding a cocktail glass than a dustpan and broom; and she emanated emotional security and an intellectual alertness still exceptional for screen wives today. In *The Great Ziegfeld*, the screwball comedy

Libeled Lady, *After the Thin Man*, all 1936, and many other immensely successful movies, Powell and Loy became firmly established as MGM's most popular screen couple, and in 1938 Loy was voted top female box office attraction. The award-winning *The Best Years of Our Lives*, 1946, elevated her to saintly status as the patient wife of war veteran Fredric March, and with halo in tow she played cameo roles right up to the seventies.

OPPOSITE: studio portrait, 1937.
Photographer Laszlo Willinger
ABOVE: *After the Thin Man*, 1936, with
William Powell and 'Asta'

61

CLAUDETTE COLBERT

If the Hollywood system was often unfair in its stereotyping of its leading ladies, a skilled ex-Broadway actress like Claudette Colbert could also be offered a surprisingly diverse choice. Just consider the bizarre contrasts in the trio of movies she made in a single year, 1934. In a welter of gems and gold she played *Cleopatra* at Paramount for Cecil B. DeMille (a sultry progression from bathing in asses' milk in his *The Sign of the Cross*, 1932). Later in the year she took the lead in *Imitation of Life*, a four-hankie weepie of a rags-to-riches white woman blind to the tragedy of her black maid. And in between these two films, she had been loaned out for four weeks to

lowly Columbia to star with Clark Gable in a comedy called *It Happened One Night*. Here Colbert walked off with the Oscar for Best Actress (Gable also took Best Actor) as the runaway heiress who teams up with a reporter on the road. Her sculpted face and delicate manners were a fine match for Gable's brusquely ribald personality, and audiences adored them. Whereas her previous roles as classical vamp or heartbroken wife traded off older attitudes, *It Happened One Night* was fresh and contemporary.

For the next ten years she was to be a major star; she was also one of the highest paid, earning over $400,000 a year from movies such as *It's a*

Wonderful World with James Stewart and *Drums Along the Mohawk*, both 1939, for John Ford. The contrast between her svelte, regal features and her talent for wacky comedy ensured that her contribution as the crazed heroine to a screwball comedy of class like Preston Sturges' *The Palm Beach Story*, 1942, would be a vital one. Colbert worked during the forties and fifties, but the pursuit of realism left her far behind.

ABOVE: publicity portrait for *Midnight*, 1939. Photographer Eugene Robert Richee

OPPOSITE: publicity portrait for *Letty Lynton*, 1932. Photographer George Hurrell

Joan Crawford survived everything. She was a star for fifty years, and she seemed able to rise above all the irrelevancies of hack plots, her ham acting and the bad reviews. It was more important to her that audiences loved her — and they did so in their thousands throughout the many phases in Crawford's career, involving change after change to her looks and hairstyle. She had been a silent Jazz Baby in the twenties, a Working-Class Girl Making Good in the early thirties, MGM Glamour Queen in the late thirties, and Washed-Up Star by the early forties. Yet, with the Oscar-winning success of *Mildred Pierce*,

RIGHT: *The Taxi Dancer*, 1927, with Owen Moore
BELOW: publicity portrait for *Grand Hotel*, 1932.
Photographer George Hurrell

1945, the quintessential Crawford movie, she bounced back from the ropes to start afresh in the post-war era. She became a late-forties Career Woman, a camp Bitch Goddess of the fifties, and, after *Whatever Happened to Baby Jane?*, 1962, metamorphosed into the Monstrous Gorgon, her last disguise and the one for which she is ironically best remembered. 'Poor Joan', as one of her fan-magazine headlines might have put it. For somewhere between the bright-eyed flapper girl of *Our Dancing Daughters*, 1928, and the grotesque portrait of her as a real-life Cruella De Ville in *Mommie Dearest*, 1981, is the story of

LEFT: studio portrait, c. 1932.
  Photographer George Hurrell
BELOW: *Strange Cargo*, 1940, with Clark Gable

a twentieth-century American woman devoured by the single thing she loved most – stardom.

Crawford's ruthless ambition was evident from the beginning. She was born as Lucille Fay Le Sueur in San Antonio, Texas, and had worked as a Kansas City shopgirl and waitress, a Chicago dancer and a Detroit chorus girl before she arrived in Hollywood aged twenty-one, doubling for Norma Shearer. Her name was changed, in Crawford's case via a nationwide publicity contest, and after hoofing it through several good-time epics, *Our Dancing Daughters* put that new name in lights. Through *Paid*, 1930, a debut with Clark Gable in *Possessed*, 1931, and alongside Garbo as a typist-on-the-make in *Grand Hotel*, 1932, Crawford found a niche as everyone's favourite working girl. Despite a failure in the dramatic role of Sadie Thompson in *Rain*, 1932, she went on to grab better roles for herself in *Dancing Lady*, 1933, opposite Gable, and in a series of star vehicles from *Today We Live*, 1933, to *The Last of Mrs Cheyney*, 1937.

Throughout the thirties Crawford's features peered out regularly from the covers of the fan magazines and women's weeklies, and in 1938, when she was voted 'box office poison' by US exhibitors, MGM could counter-attack by saying that Crawford had received a phenomenal total of 900,000 fan letters. (Some contemporary Hollywood wits said they could imagine Crawford counting every one.) If familiarity had bred contempt by then, with Frank Borzage's *Mannequin*, 1937, and especially with Cukor's *The Women*, 1939, Crawford proved that there were directors in Hollywood who could profitably exploit her tough glamour, brittle passions and vivid sense of melodrama. But after two more years MGM let her go free-lance. She signed up with Warners,

ABOVE: studio portrait, c. 1935.
Photographer George Hurrell
RIGHT: *Chained*, 1934, with Clark Gable
OPPOSITE: studio portrait, 1935.
Photographer George Hurrell

but had to plead with them for the lead in the *film noir* melodrama *Mildred Pierce*. As a housewife sacrificing herself for her spiteful and thankless daughter, Crawford played the part of her life with a wide-eyed zeal that was awesome. Her face was harder, fiercer than before, with a mouth painted like a clown's; her prize of an Oscar must have seemed sweet revenge.

Humoresque, 1946, *Flamingo Road*, 1949, and *This Woman is Dangerous*, 1952, all proved that she was in her prime, her face portraying renewed passion and determination with the fixed intensity of an eastern goddess. Even in the highlights of her fifties career, such as the baroque operatic Western, *Johnny Guitar*, 1954, Crawford seemed to inhabit a different

plane to her co-stars, who could only cower in her presence. It was as if she had been taken over by a demon power, and Robert Aldrich used that not-so-latent quality of madness to great effect in the riveting *Whatever Happened to Baby Jane?* With less sure direction, that same quality also produced cheap trash like *Berserk*, 1967, and *Trog*, 1970, two films in which Crawford's image came very close indeed to the sinister harridan portrayed in *Mommie Dearest*, her daughter's vengeful biography of her.

F. Scott Fitzgerald once wrote of her, 'She can't change her emotions in the middle of a scene without going through a sort of Jekyll and Hyde contortion of the face.' But she did show that cinema acting is not so much a

question of dramatic subtlety as one of sheer presence and charisma – even if, at times, one cannot quite be sure that she is actually acting at all.

ABOVE: *Above Suspicion*, 1943, with Fred MacMurray

Neglected and unfashionable though she undoubtedly is, it's still possible to have a soft spot for Irene Dunne, if only in one of her guises as 'queen of the weepies'. Trained as an opera singer, and a seasoned stage performer, she was in fact an extremely versatile actress, switching from musicals to melodrama and comedy without showing signs of strain, and she remained a top star for different studios until the late 1940s, receiving no less than five Academy Award nominations along the way.

She established herself in a thundering Western, *Cimarron*, 1931, for which she was Oscar nominated, and was later to repeat her stage role as Magnolia in the musical *Show Boat*, 1936; but it was the vogue for the 'woman's picture' which really launched her. In *Back Street*, 1932, Dunne showed a capacity for saint-like suffering that was truly awesome. John Boles played a respectable banker, and she his secret mistress, and Dunne showed a cheery face in great adversity. In *Magnificent Obsession*, 1935, directed by the same man, John M. Stahl, Dunne played an attractive widow accidentally blinded by a pretty-faced playboy (Robert Taylor). Masochistic wallowing in oppression was, of course, nothing new, but Dunne brought such conviction to her performance that her extremes of anguish swayed even hardened cynics. She remained extremely adaptable. She turned to screwball comedy in *Theodora Goes Wild*, 1936, with Melvyn Douglas, and clowned with Cary Grant in the following year in *The Awful Truth*. Her leading roles in *Joy of Living*, 1938, opposite Douglas Fairbanks Jr, and *Love Affair*, 1939, opposite the dashing Charles Boyer, carried her into another decade as a top star who was also a studio boss's dream: popular, tame, and able to play leading roles in both comedy and drama with equal aplomb.

RIGHT: publicity portrait for *Roberta*, 1935.
Photographer Ernest A. Bachrach

LORETTA YOUNG

With her apple cheeks, full lips and cat eyes, Loretta Young possessed a traditional beauty which nonetheless appears with hindsight more like an identikit image, a sort of detective's sketch of a Hollywood ideal which sheds little light on anything real. Behind those limpid pools is . . . perhaps not very much. Such niceties did not prevent her from rising to stardom in a series of roles as downtrodden working girls, and she was resourceful enough to become known somewhat disrespectfully – and unfairly – as 'Hollywood's beautiful hack'.

Aged fifteen, she got her first bit part by taking a phone call for her sister, already an actress, from director Mervyn LeRoy. It led to starring roles before she was twenty, and her most exciting work stems from this period: as a rival reporter to Harlow in *Platinum Blonde*, 1931, as wife to James Cagney in *Taxi*, 1932, in *Zoo in Budapest*, 1933, and in Frank Borzage's melodrama *A Man's Castle*, also 1933, in which Spencer Tracy saves her from a fate as a prostitute. She was adaptable enough to star opposite such varied leading men as Conrad Nagel, Ronald Colman, Cary Grant, Charles Boyer, Henry Wilcoxon, Tyrone Power and Robert Taylor. But she seemed unwilling to settle down with one studio – she hopped around between Warners, Paramount, 20th Century Fox and Columbia and didn't care to develop a niche for herself. Her star status was from the late 1940s not always assured, but she nevertheless bounced back to win an Oscar in an unlikely comedy, *The Farmer's Daughter*, 1947. By 1953 she had departed for a television drama series: perhaps her bland beauty had at last found its natural home.

LEFT: off set *Midnight Mary*, 1933

ABOVE: publicity portrait for *Shanghai Express*, 1932.
Photographer Don English

Dietrich herself would have it that the world's first glimpse of her was on her entrance in *Der blaue Engel/The Blue Angel*, 1930. As the teasing vamp Lola Lola she perched tantalizingly on stage, held out her long stocking-clad legs for approval, tilted her mannish top hat rakishly to one side, and delivered a rendition of 'Falling in Love Again' with such languorous eroticism that, in James Agate's memorable phrase, she seemed to make 'reason totter on her throne'. As she enslaved the hapless schoolteacher Emil Jannings to her every whim, she created a seductively androgynous fantasy female that was the great achievement of herself and director Josef von

Sternberg, during the six films they made together for Paramount over the following years.

It mattered little that this 'new Garbo' was already in her late twenties and the mother of a five-year-old daughter, nor that she had been appearing in movies since 1923. For the Dietrich myth was, from the very moment that Sternberg saw her performing on stage, a monument to elaborate artifice and teasing ambiguity. In *Morocco*, 1930, *Dishonored*, 1931, *Shanghai Express*, 1932, *Blonde Venus*, 1932, *The Scarlet Empress*, 1934, and *The Devil is a Woman*, 1935, she, Sternberg and cinematographers Lee Garmes and

71

Bert Glennon perfected a Dietrich who was an elusive and exotic figment of the imagination. Swathed in veils and feathers, criss-crossed in patterns of light, she was as beguiling and inaccessible as a goddess. Compared with Garbo's realism, Dietrich was intended as a figure of illusion, beyond belief and as magical as the flickering image of cinema itself. She rightfully belonged in the Paramount-style *demi-monde* of Morocco or Shanghai, where her siren qualities could lure in every bar-room Ulysses like Gary Cooper or Clive Brook who should stumble unsuspectingly upon her.

RIGHT: studio portrait, 1930.
        Photographer Eugene Robert Richee
BELOW: *The Garden of Allah*, 1936, with
        Charles Boyer

Dietrich and Sternberg experimented as she grew in popularity, and adorned her body in an increasingly fetishistic manner. Her masculine appearance in top hat and tails or men's suits lent an intriguing sexual ambiguity to her persona, and set a fashion in the early thirties that evoked a vague reminder of Weimar decadence and perversity. She was merely a cabaret singer for *Morocco*, but became a Mata Hari-type spy clad in black leather for *Dishonored*; and as the infamous Shanghai Lily in *Shanghai Express* she draped herself in feather boas and veils. *The Scarlet Empress*

LEFT: publicity portrait for *Shanghai Express*, 1932.
Photographer Don English
BELOW: *Blonde Venus*, 1932, with Cary Grant

allowed her to indulge in the extravagantly regal costumes of Catherine the Great, and in *Blonde Venus* and *The Devil is a Woman* she became increasingly immobile under a bewildering array of wigs, slit skirts, shimmering dresses and even a gorilla suit. These disguises knowingly aroused desires which her character proceeded to dismiss with contempt. For her persona was built around the supremely romantic notion that love is impossible. She lived in a never-changing world of obsession and devotion — a long way indeed from the Hollywood ideal of cosy married bliss.

Disappointing box office returns for *The Devil is a Woman* reduced Paramount's confidence in their actor–director partnership, and it was to be Dietrich's last film with Von Sternberg. Her career now slid dramatically. Even directors like Frank Borzage (*Desire*, 1936) or Ernst Lubitsch (*Angel*, 1937) could not recapture her magic. She dropped to 126th place in the box office polls, and Paramount bought out her contract. They had tried to use her as an actress, but her technique had been misunderstood. She was actually the charismatic central figure of an aesthetic, and could no more adapt to a different style than a statue can alter its pose.

Dietrich did return in a comic role in *Destry Rides Again*, 1939, was admired by both John Wayne and Randolph Scott in *Spoilers*, 1942, and recovered some of her old exoticism when she was painted gold for *Kismet*, 1944. During the war she entertained US troops and made anti-Nazi propaganda broadcasts in her native German, but as an actress she remained under-used until 1948, when Billy Wilder's *A Foreign Affair* set her in the ruins of Berlin after the war. By then she had adopted a new career as a *chanteuse*, and her legendary nightclub

LEFT: publicity photograph for *Shanghai Express*, 1932, with and by photographer Don English
OPPOSITE: studio portrait, 1935. Photographer Eugene Robert Richee

act resurrected again and again the memory of the thirties Dietrich – even if she herself tetchily dismissed those early movies of hers. She has returned to films only infrequently, most tellingly in Orson Welles' *Touch of Evil*, 1958, in which she somehow played the madame of a Mexican saloon with effortless conviction. *Judgment at Nuremberg*, 1961, could be justified, but *Schöner Gigolo – Armer Gigolo/ Just a Gigolo*, 1978, could not: it was a disappointing full stop to a movie career that had effectively halted more than forty years ago.

RIGHT: portrait, 1935.
　　　Photographer Eugene Robert Richee
BELOW: *Destry Rides Again*, 1939, with
　　　James Stewart

Tall and commanding, confident and poised, Rosalind Russell made her name in Hollywood's favourite vogue role of the thirties and forties – as the career woman. She recalled that she played a career woman on screen at least twenty-three times, owning everything from factories and advertising agencies to pharmaceutical houses. 'Except for leading men and a switch in title and pompadour,' she once reminisced, 'they were all stamped out of the same Alice in Careerland. My wardrobe had a set pattern: a tan suit, a grey suit, a beige suit, and then a negligee for the seventh reel, near the end, when I would admit to my best friend on the telephone that what I really wanted was to become a dear little housewife.'

All this was, however, a successful progression from her early Hollywood roles at MGM between 1934 and 1939, where she was most often cast as the second woman to a Jean Harlow or a Maureen O'Sullivan. But in her first film as a freelance player she more than made up for it. As ace news reporter Hildy Johnson in Howard Hawks' *His Girl Friday*, 1940, she is the only woman in the press pool and gives that particular career girl an enviable line in cynical repartee. She outwits her scheming editor Walter Burns (Cary Grant) by trading wisecracks at breakneck speed in her all-time best role as 'one of the guys'. Maybe it wasn't matched by her roles in *No Time for Comedy*, also 1940, with James Stewart, or *This Thing Called Love*, 1941, with Melvyn Douglas, but then it would have been hard for anyone to top. Nominated four times for an Academy Award – the last was for *Auntie Mame*, 1958 – her stage career took up most of her time after the forties, with only occasional forays back to Hollywood.

RIGHT: studio portrait, c. 1936

CONSTANCE BENNETT

Second only to Garbo as a box office star in the early thirties, and known for a short while as the 'highest-paid woman in Hollywood', Constance Bennett is neglected and unfashionable today. Naturally sleek and elegant rather than gawky or brash, she sums up an old-fashioned quality of charm, from her arched eyebrows to the way she holds a cigarette. She has all the screen finesse of an actress trained as a silent star, and her career was to progress through at least three contrasting stages from the early 1920s.

Bennett made a name as a flirtatious flapper as early as 1925 in *The Goose Hangs High*, but when she married a young millionaire in 1926 she went into a period of retirement, aged twenty-two. (This was already her second marriage.) Tearjerking hits such as *Common Clay*, 1930, and *What Price Hollywood?*, 1932, marked her return to Hollywood and her debut in the talkies, and during these years Bennett became master of the role of the downtrodden martyr. Despite her sophistication and off-screen marriage to the Marquis de Falaise de la Coudraye (ex-husband of Swanson and an executive at MGM) – or perhaps because of these things – everyone seemed to love her playing characters at the very bottom of the social scale. Nevertheless, Bennett's high gloss and innate worldly wisdom were probably better exploited in her best-remembered roles as a husky-voiced, wisecracking light comedienne: in the ingenious *Topper*, 1937, she plays a ghost with Cary Grant, and in the screwball comedy *Merrily We Live*, 1938, she is a rich girl who falls for her down-and-out chauffeur, Brian Aherne. Bennett was perfect for that period of innocent, glamorous refinement, but her popularity did not outlast the decade: Constance's younger sister Joan landed better roles than she in the 1940s, and Constance left for the stage early in the fifties.

LEFT: studio portrait, 1933.
Photographer Ernest A. Bachrach

JOAN BENNETT

As the dark-haired beauty of a trio of Fritz Lang movies – *Man Hunt*, 1941, *The Woman in the Window*, 1944, and *Scarlet Street*, 1946 – Joan Bennett carved herself a niche as an alluring *femme fatale*, a treacherous but bewitching siren with curled lip and slit skirt. Together with her roles as devious deceiver in Jean Renoir's *The Woman on the Beach*, 1947, as the terrified young bride in Fritz Lang's *Secret Beyond the Door*, 1948, and as the desperate mother facing up to James Mason's blackmail in Max Ophüls' *The Reckless Moment*, 1949, her career adds up to a vintage collection of studies in the twists of fate, of security suddenly turned into nightmarish uncertainty. These were the most illustrious roles in a career that had its own reckless moments.

As younger sister of the famous Constance Bennett, and also a blonde, Joan had a lot of catching up to do. She grew up fast. By the time she was eighteen, Joan had eloped with a millionaire, had his child and been divorced. She began acting regularly in the movies in 1928, and soon built a career for herself with strong roles in George Cukor's *Little Women*, 1933, and with Bing Crosby in *Mississippi* and *Two for Tonight*, both 1935. But her fortunes changed dramatically when she donned a black wig for *Trade Winds*, 1939, and in 1940 she married producer Walter Wanger (her third husband), under whose supervision she was really to make her mark. Joan became a favourite dark lady, surrounded by an aura of mystery and brooding passions that her blonde persona had lacked. Wanger claimed it was jealousy that made him shoot her agent, Jennings Lang, in the early fifties; he served a jail sentence for it, and although he and Bennett teamed back up when he was released, they divorced in 1965. By that time Joan had followed her sister on to the stage and into television.

RIGHT: studio portrait, 1937.
Photographer Ernest A. Bachrach

OLIVIA DE HAVILLAND

Sweet and dainty, steadfast and demure, Olivia De Havilland was the ideal romantic foil for the roguish Errol Flynn in a long series of Warner Bros. swashbucklers. She was forever the faithful sweetheart, with an eye-fluttering innocence which seemed to belong to the bygone age in which so many of her adventures were set. In *Captain Blood*, 1935, and *The Charge of the Light Brigade*, 1936, as Maid Marion in *The Adventures of Robin Hood*, 1938, and as Bette Davis' maid-of-honour rival in *The Private Lives of Elizabeth and Essex*, 1939, she inhabited a fairy-tale world in which men were valiant and she was always legal, decent, honest and true.

Born of British parents, De Havilland grew up in California with her younger sister Joan Fontaine. Warners signed her up after her appearance as Hermia in the stage and film versions of 'A Midsummer Night's Dream'. The apogee of her goody-goody image came as Melanie in *Gone With the Wind*, 1939, but the belief in her character marked a skilled actress at work. After better roles as James Cagney's wife in *The Strawberry Blonde*, 1941, and as a wronged spinster at the hands of the cynical Charles Boyer in *Hold Back the Dawn*, 1941, for which she won an Oscar nomination, she was ready to expand her range. She fought Warners through the courts to win freedom from a seven-year contract, and celebrated by winning two Best Actress Oscars for *To Each His Own*, 1946, and *The Heiress*, 1949. The truest moments of her career came in an eerie double role in *The Dark Mirror*, 1946, in which she played twin sisters, one good, one evil: it was as if, after all those years, the butter had finally begun to melt in her mouth.

OPPOSITE: studio portrait, c. 1941.
   Photographer Scotty Welbourne
ABOVE: *The Private Lives of Elizabeth and Essex*, 1939, with Errol Flynn
RIGHT: publicity portrait for *Raffles*, 1940, with David Niven

DOROTHY LAMOUR

When the US marines were fighting in the South Pacific, they perhaps dreamt of finding a native girl with all the attributes of Dorothy Lamour: olive-skinned but only slightly slant-eyed, her body draped in a skimpy sarong, her voice half-way between the sultriness of a Bali goddess and the wise-cracks of a big city bargirl. She was the home-from-home figure at the end of the Roads to *Singapore*, 1940, *Zanzibar*, 1941, *Morocco*, 1942, *Utopia*, 1945, *Rio*, 1947, and *Bali*, 1952, confronted with lust and confusion in equal parts by Bob Hope and Bing Crosby. Hope, with crossed eyes, fumbling fingers and tied tongue, realized by proxy every soldier's dreams – every soldier, that is, who ever fostered secret fantasies about desert island Crusoes and Lamouresque Girl Fridays.

Despite her patriotic sporting of the sarong, it is easy to believe Lamour when she said it was more like a strait-jacket. She did get to play gun molls, singers and more dramatic roles on occasion, but still the public clamoured for her as the unclaimed mistress of the South Seas. So half-dressed and exotic was how Paramount liked to keep her. In her scenes with Bob Hope, she plays a wily and knowing girl, fending off the feeble attentions of this love-crazed incompetent; although the high drama is scarce on the ground, to say the least, Lamour's effortless playing of light comedy, to the point of self-parody, still raises the necessary laughter. 'Miss New Orleans' of 1931, Lamour had first come to Hollywood's attention as a singer, and retired to that profession; when she returned for one last escapade on *The Road to Hong Kong*, 1961, it was as a guest star, her place now occupied by the very unexotic Joan Collins.

LEFT: studio portrait, 1938.
     Photographer William Walling Jr

OPPOSITE: studio portrait, 1936.
     Photographer Ernest A. Bachrach

The prevailing wisdom that Katharine Hepburn was never considered conventionally beautiful seems perverse. Certainly her high cheekbones, piercing eyes and flashing smile are of a different order to both Garbo's exoticism or Harlow's dimestore platinum blonde, if they are taken as the two extremes of thirties glamour. Hepburn is uniquely East Coast establishment, the proud and confident daughter of a wealthy Connecticut family, an actress whose Bryn Mawr College accent sounded a novel note in Hollywood. Certainly her quality of refined intelligence belied a reputation as a mere

RIGHT: *The Philadelphia Story*, 1940, with
James Stewart
BELOW: *Sylvia Scarlett*, 1935, with Brian Aherne

'beauty'. But perhaps the reason was simpler even than this: here was a fêted Broadway actress whose early movie roles won her popular success, critical acclaim and a brace of Oscar nominations, as well as rumours of an engagement to mogul Howard Hughes. It may just have been too galling for Hollywood gossips to admit that, with all this, Hepburn was actually *beautiful* too.

The movie colony's reaction to her was certainly peculiar. Her earliest starring roles for RKO were all hits: *A Bill of Divorcement*, 1932, *Morning Glory* (for which she won an Oscar) and *Little Women*, both 1933. Roles like

LEFT: *Undercurrent*, 1946, with Robert Taylor
BELOW: *Bringing Up Baby*, 1938

ABOVE: studio portrait, 1936.
Photographer Ernest A. Bachrach
OPPOSITE: publicity portrait for *Bringing Up Baby*,
1938, with Cary Grant.
Photographer Ernest A. Bachrach

the aviatrix *Christopher Strong*, 1933, and the androgynous *Sylvia Scarlett*, 1935, established her as an unorthodox and independent actress with the same scornful disdain for Hollywood etiquette that she had had for Broadway etiquette in an earlier stage of her career. Yet the prestigious *Quality Street*, 1937, was a failure, and not even her classic comic lead opposite Cary Grant in *Bringing Up Baby*, 1938, could bring her back to favour. Her RKO period came to an end, and, like Joan Crawford, she was labelled 'box office poison' by exhibitors – as if no-one had ever laughed at the sight of her trying to control a leopard on a leash in one of Hepburn and Grant's more bizarre comic moments.

The Philadelphia Story, 1940, brought her back to Hollywood and MGM with an Oscar nomination, a smash hit and a mint of money, for on her return to Broadway she had starred in and picked up the film rights to this hugely popular comedy. As an elegant heiress opposite James Stewart and Cary Grant, Hepburn excels at sophisticated banter, alternately as flirtatious as a kitten and stuffily severe. She was in her prime. When MGM teamed her for the first time with Spencer Tracy in *Woman of the Year*, 1942, their chemistry was immediately apparent. They were complete opposites. Tracy appeared bullish, instinctive, quietly sly; Hepburn was strong-willed, fiery, cleverly talkative. They excelled in battles of the sexes, and transformed the on-screen duels of *State of the Union*, 1948, *Adam's Rib*, 1949, and *Pat and Mike*, 1952, into an off-screen relationship of lasting affection. They never married (Tracy would not insist

on a divorce from his wife), but their partnership was an open secret for the rest of their lives.

Hepburn managed both to astonish Bogart in *The African Queen*, 1951, and win another Oscar nomination. Although her liberated image now tended towards overtly spinsterish roles, films like *Summer Madness*, 1955, *The Rainmaker*, 1956, *Suddenly Last Summer*, 1959, and especially *Long Day's Journey Into Night*, 1962, all benefited from her presence. If the fifties was a busy decade for her, she spent five years from 1962 away from stage or screen, nursing a dying father and seriously ill Tracy. The famous pair returned for *Guess Who's Coming to Dinner*, 1967, Tracy's last film. It won her an Oscar, as did *The Lion in Winter*, 1968, with Peter O'Toole, and later *On Golden Pond*, 1981, with Henry Fonda. She encouraged sympathy and admiration from both critics and audience, even if her acting had long since drifted into mannerism.

Nobody cared, since Hepburn had not only consistently justified her position at the top of her profession, but had also come to be recognized as a truly emancipated woman, one who was just as in tune with the post-sixties world of Jane Fonda and Vanessa Redgrave as with the Hollywood establishment of which she was so much a part. Her mother had been a suffragette and early supporter of birth control, and some of that tough, New England-style radicalism managed to permeate the tinseltown glamour in which Hepburn was perpetually shrouded. As the jaded sophisticate, daring aviatrix, screwball comic, shrewd careerist or battling spinster, Hepburn never let go of that inheritance. All that, and beautiful too.

ABOVE: studio portrait, 1941.
     Photographer Clarence Sinclair Bull
RIGHT: publicity portrait for *Without Love*, 1945,
     with Spencer Tracy.
     Photographer Clarence Sinclair Bull

Astaire and Rogers in motion were a
blissful union. She was bubbly, brash,
colourful, real-life; he was cool,
dapper, black and white, abstract. As
cheek to cheek they glide over those
gleaming floors, love and romance
seem to come to life on the screen,
eclipsing the real world and making it
seem tawdry and irrelevant. In ten
classic movies with Astaire, reaching
its acme with *Swing Time*, 1936,
Rogers sparkles like a bright gem,
adding visible warmth and humanity to
the austere brilliance of Astaire.

The vaudeville circuit was the first
stop on Rogers' rise to stardom, and
from there she got work for various
film studios. There was a quality of
toughness about Rogers, even in her
films with Astaire, that served her well
in this period, in her roles as a gum-
chewing, wisecracking broad: she
was one of the girls sharing a world-
weary giggle in Warner's *42nd Street*,
1933, and an eager cynic in a go-
getting world in *Gold Diggers of 1933*.
Her next major film was at RKO, and
with Astaire; but in 1939 after *The
Story of Vernon and Irene Castle*,
Rogers went her own way. She quickly
proved her professionalism in *Kitty
Foyle*, 1940, for which she won the
Best Actress Oscar: as a salesgirl who
lands a rich man, but who begins to
hanker after one of her own kind, the
role is a good example of Rogers'
appeal to young girls of her own class.
Rogers was best in comedy, as when
she breezily holds a court to ransom
with her sob story and hitched-up skirt
as *Roxie Hart*, 1942. Her film career
continued throughout the fifties, and
she had great success both on Broadway and the London stage in the
sixties. But she never found as complementary a leading man as Astaire.
Apart, they each graduated to their
respective worlds; but together, they
defined romance.

RIGHT: publicity portrait for *Once Upon a
   Honeymoon*, 1942, with Cary Grant.
   Photographer John Miehle

MERLE OBERON

Whenever Merle Oberon is seen as Cathy in *Wuthering Heights*, 1939, she never leaves a dry eye in the house. Opposite Laurence Olivier's Heathcliff, she seems to ebb and swell with passion until her heart breaks; and it is only after seeing it many times that one begins to notice the Californian sets, the truncated and perfunctory script and, indeed, Oberon's own weaknesses. But no matter that her speech is polite and characterless: her frail physique and imploring eyes do more on screen than many more talented thespians could manage.

Born in India, Oberon was to carve out a peripatetic career for herself on both sides of the Atlantic. In England in 1933 producer and future husband Alexander Korda first gave her a break with the part of Anne Boleyn in *The Private Life of Henry VIII*. After a lead opposite Leslie Howard in the extravagant costumes of *The Scarlet Pimpernel*, 1935, she was in demand everywhere; but a bad accident set a temporary halt to her career and a permanent one to Korda's *I, Claudius*, which she was making at the time. Though Korda's influence guided her throughout the thirties and early forties (they divorced in 1945), she was much more than his successful protégé. In 1935 Korda had sold a share of her contract to Sam Goldwyn, and thereafter she commuted between London and Hollywood. Perhaps Korda's predilection for historical pomp inhibited her transition to more modern circumstances, for certainly her contemporary roles left much to be desired. Her screen appearances in the fifties were sporadic, and even by the time she made *Berlin Express* in 1948, her career was visibly on the decline. Her previous associations with more grandiose leading men made a square-jawed *homme ordinaire* like Dana Andrews look like a demotion.

OPPOSITE: studio portrait, 1944.
        Photographer Robert W. Coburn
ABOVE: *The Scarlet Pimpernel*, 1935, with
        Leslie Howard
LEFT: *Beloved Enemy*, 1936, with David Niven

91

PAULETTE GODDARD

Everyone loved Paulette Goddard's grin. Charlie Chaplin saw her as a bewitching *gamine*, fell in love and married her (secretly, at sea, at some time in the mid-thirties); his children wrote about how they saw rare qualities in her and adored her smile. She was probably wearing that famous grin when she left the Ziegfeld chorus line in her late teens to marry a millionaire. Just a few years later, divorced and with $500,000 alimony, she arrived in Hollywood. When she met Chaplin she was already a rich woman, an aspiring actress, and glamorously blonde; when she left him in the early 1940s, she was a brunette, even richer, and one of Paramount's leading stars.

Her roles in Chaplin's *Modern Times*, 1936, and *The Great Dictator*, 1940, are her claims to posterity, and she manages a rare kinship on screen with a man who usually entirely dominated the proceedings. But it was her aura of capriciousness and lively spirit which made her a front runner for the part of Scarlett O'Hara in *Gone With the Wind* until Vivien Leigh appeared on the scene. As if in compensation, she played the leading Southern belle in DeMille's epic *Reap the Wild Wind*, 1942, and firmly established herself as one of Paramount's top stars. Her best role was as the coquettish lead in Jean Renoir's *Diary of a Chambermaid*, 1946, in which everybody fell in love with her, including her real-life husband at the time, Burgess Meredith. Even when compared with Jeanne Moreau in the same role nearly two decades later, Goddard exudes a confident allure which is just right. Soon after that, her career came to an end. She has come out of her luxurious retirement with her fourth husband only once, in 1964, when she made *Gli Indifferenti/Time of Indifference* with Claudia Cardinale.

ABOVE: *Modern Times*, 1936, with
    Charlie Chaplin
LEFT: studio portrait, 1932.
    Photographer Clarence Sinclair Bull

For a brief while Hedy Lamarr was proclaimed as the successor to Garbo. Billed by MGM's Louis B. Mayer as 'the most beautiful woman in films', Lamarr was given the full benefit of the MGM publicity machine just as Garbo herself was proving awkward to handle and faltering at the box office. Lamarr certainly projected a distinct, exotic glamour that passed off as vaguely 'European'. But she lacked a distinct charisma or personality to match her beauty. When Mayer realized that this 'next Garbo' was fool's gold, he began to lose interest, particularly since she too was proving difficult to please: she turned down the leads in *Casablanca, Gaslight* and *Saratoga Trunk*, and left the field clear for Ingrid Bergman.

Lamarr had been discovered in Berlin by Max Reinhardt, so the story goes, and achieved notoriety in a Czech film, *Extase*, of 1933. The young Hedwig Kiesler (her real name) was glimpsed running naked through a sylvan glade. A buzz of excitement greeted this artistic performance, which rose to a salacious frenzy when the film was shown in the USA. With prudish reservations Mayer signed this new star, but nervously leased her out to another producer, Walter Wanger. Everything augured well with her first leading role in *Algiers*, 1938, as a bewitching temptress who lures Charles Boyer out of the casbah. But despite the sterling efforts of such slogans as 'You too will be "Hedy" with delight and your verdict will be "Lamarrvellous"', her follow-ups generally failed to sparkle.

She was given every inducement: Spencer Tracy for *I Take This Woman*, 1939, Clark Gable for *Boom Town* and *Comrade X*, both 1940, not to mention other leading men like James Stewart, Robert Taylor, Walter Pidgeon and William Powell. *Ziegfeld Girl*, 1941, in which she co-starred with Judy Garland and Lana Turner, remains one of her most entertaining efforts.

RIGHT: studio portrait, 1939.
Photographer Laszlo Willinger

She achieved her finest hour — and her biggest box office hit — in DeMille's gaudy Biblical epic *Samson and Delilah*, 1949, opposite Victor Mature, whose own caricatured good looks and acting prowess were wholly in her own class. Lamarr portrayed Delilah with a healthy disregard for any attempt at realism. Her determination and panache helped make it a box office hit, and amid the ruins of its Technicolor temple, it could be said that she had found her true level at last.

RIGHT: publicity portrait for *Lady of the Tropics*, 1939.
       Photographer Laszlo Willinger
BELOW: publicity portrait for *Lady of the Tropics*,
       1939, with Robert Taylor.
       Photographer Clarence Sinclair Bull
OPPOSITE: studio portrait, 1938.
       Photographer Robert W. Coburn

BETTE DAVIS

When Bette Davis rebelled against her studio bosses at Warner Bros. in 1937, she could have been acting out a page from one of her own scripts – or at least the kind of script she *wanted* to get. This fierce, twenty-eight-year-old New Englander had fought her way from provincial theatre school into the first rank of Hollywood stars, was already considered an unparalleled movie actress with an Oscar for *Dangerous*, 1935, to prove it, and knew she was worth more than a re-hashed version of 'The Maltese Falcon', even if it was called *Satan Met a*

OPPOSITE: studio portrait, c. 1939.
Photographer George Hurrell
LEFT: studio portrait, c. 1933.
Photographer Elmer Fryer
BELOW: *The Petrified Forest*, 1936, with Leslie Howard

Lady, 1936. So she packed her bags and left for England, intending to end the battles over parts with Warners and make a movie out of contract. Warners slapped an injunction on her. She contested it. A court case followed, and the movie world held its breath. Warners were held to be legally in the right in claiming that her contract ran exclusively for another five years. But Davis was the true victor; after that nobody would push her around again.

That incident from her own life was uncannily typical of her movies. Ever since her debut in *Bad Sister*, 1931, and even as the scheming waitress in RKO's *Of Human Bondage*, 1934, she had made the tough-hearted melodrama her dominion. No matter how bad the script — and it was often really terrible — Davis managed to summon up an overpowering conviction in the material that was always her saving grace. No matter that she tended towards ham as she dished out verbal torture with unashamed relish, she always left an audience convinced of her emotional sincerity. She was for that reason alone the top screen actress of her day.

After her legal battle with Warners, her talent was more justly exploited with a succession of vintage roles, as a Southern belle in *Jezebel*, 1938, suffering a brain tumour and blindness in *Dark Victory*, 1939, madness in *Juarez*, 1939, pining for Errol Flynn in *The Private Lives of Elizabeth and Essex*, 1939, and falling in love with Charles Boyer in *All This and Heaven Too*, 1940. After shooting her lover in *The Letter*, 1940, she went from strength to strength in *The Little Foxes*, 1941, *Now, Voyager*, 1942, and *Mr Skeffington*, 1944.

After this long run of successes, *The Corn is Green*, 1945, started a series of flops. It seemed that Davis had at last

ABOVE: *Jezebel*, 1938, with Henry Fonda
RIGHT: publicity portrait for *The Little Foxes*, 1941.
  Photographer Ned Scott

out-stayed her welcome, and in 1949 she was finally released from her Warners contract. If she had vanished then, it could have been said that she thrived best on the welter of hidden emotions of those uncertain war years, and that America in peacetime was unsympathetic to her acid personality. However, no-one reckoned with *All About Eve*, 1950, when Davis took over from Claudette Colbert as the vitriolic Margo Channing. In retrospect, it seems absurd that anyone else but Davis should have been approached to play the spitefully bitchy, but absolutely charming, Margo. The dialogue flew from Davis' mouth like poisoned darts, and she proved, once again, that she was indeed a force to be reckoned with.

Perhaps it was not her fault if Davis' movies after *The Virgin Queen*, 1955, failed to live up to her earlier successes. Some would blame it on her own egotism, others on timidity on the part of the studios. Nevertheless Davis was to pull more surprises out of the hat. *Whatever Happened to Baby Jane?*, 1962, allowed her to exercise freely that talent for Grand Guignol that had never been far beneath her acting style. It was an unexpected success. In both this and its follow-up, *Hush . . . Hush Sweet Charlotte*, 1964, she surprised critics and public by her sincere conviction, a conviction that spilled over into less subtle, more camp offerings like *The Nanny*, 1965, and *The Anniversary*, 1967. In her autobiography *The Lonely Life* published in 1962 Davis declared, 'I'll never make the mistake of saying I'm retired. You do that and you're finished. You just have to make sure you play older and older parts. Hell, I could do a million of those character roles. But I'm stubborn about playing the lead. I'd like to go out with my name above the title.' Movie stars don't come much older than Bette Davis; now well into her

ABOVE: *The Great Lie*, 1941, with George Brent
LEFT: publicity portrait for *The Letter*, 1940.
Photographer George Hurrell

eighties her sinewy body is worn and frail but her powerhouse mind seems as determined as ever. Even in *Death on the Nile*, 1978, she managed to spit some life into the kind of star vehicle she used to drive single-handed in the good old days, when her strength and vitality were at their peak.

OPPOSITE: publicity portrait for *Dark Victory*, 1939.
LEFT: publicity portrait for *Now, Voyager*, 1942. Photographer Bert Six
Photographer George Hurrell
BELOW: *All About Eve*, 1950, with Gary Merrill

GREER GARSON

Greer Garson is forever *Mrs Miniver*, that saintly wartime madonna who nobly suffered the worst that the Nazis could fling at her country. Gazing out at the night-time skies in the arms of husband Walter Pidgeon, she is the very symbol of British resistance: moral, defiant, stiff-upper-lipped, with a self-deprecating sense of humour that charms the most cynical. Her performance in that film is said to have done more to shift American public opinion on to Britain's side in World War Two than any other single thing; her Best Actress Oscar, one of six nominations in seven years, was amply deserved.

In many ways Garson was an actress from a previous age, in the tradition of Norma Shearer (who had turned down the Miniver role). Her first costume role – and her third film – was as Elizabeth Bennett in *Pride and Prejudice*, 1940, opposite Laurence Olivier; and after the success of *Mrs Miniver* in 1942 it was roles iike *Madame Curie*, 1944, opposite Walter Pidgeon again, that came her way. Both Shearer and Garson possessed a matronly calm, but both lacked that exuberant punch that might have enabled adaptation to less regal roles. Garson nevertheless enjoyed phenomenal popularity, and her record of Oscar nominations is still unmatched. Her reign during the 1940s was backed to the hilt by Louis B. Mayer, who had personally spotted her before the war on the London stage; his support was more than justified by hits like *Random Harvest*, 1942, with Ronald Colman, and *The Valley of Decision*, 1945. With the end of the war, however, Garson's popularity began to fade; for from her film debut as the wife in *Goodbye, Mr Chips*, 1939, she had been synonymous with the qualities of virtuous, wifely self-sacrifice which had struck so powerful and so unique a chord with wartime audiences.

LEFT: publicity portrait for *Goodbye, Mr Chips*, 1939.
Photographer Davis Boulton

MARGARET LOCKWOOD　ANNA NEAGLE

Imperious, nostalgic, anodyne, wooden, Dame Anna Neagle triumphed as Britain's top box office draw for years, and with director (later husband) Herbert Wilcox, invented an entire tradition of British womanhood from the youthful *Nell Gwyn*, 1934, to *Victoria the Great*, 1937. Neagle's cycle of London dramas with Michael Wilding (*Piccadilly Incident, The Courtneys of Curzon Street, Spring in Park Lane* and *Maytime in Mayfair*, all 1946–9) was never less than cloyingly sentimental, not to say snobbish. Graham Greene found cause to remark on her inexpressiveness: she was 'rather like a mechanical marvel from the World's Fair'. Synonymous to Britons with the dark days of rationing, her career declined in the fifties.

BELOW: *Spring in Park Lane*, 1948, with Michael Wilding

Margaret Lockwood blossomed opposite sneering villains like James Mason and Stewart Granger into the very epitome of wickedness. Briefly ranked as one of Britain's top movie stars, she was to have her finest hour in *The Wicked Lady*, 1945, in which she played a double-dealing murderess with heaving bosom and cruel smile. In her films of the early forties Lockwood managed to suggest an inner madness behind a svelte exterior, an image that marked a distinct change in intensity from her pre-war roles: of these the most famous had been opposite Michael Redgrave in Hitchcock's *The Lady Vanishes*, and in *Bank Holiday*, both 1938. Her star waned with the forties, and she mellowed sweetly.

ABOVE: publicity portrait for *The Wicked Lady*, 1945, with James Mason. Photographer Ted Reed

VIVIEN LEIGH

It is puzzling, to say the least, that an eminent British stage actress should come to scoop two of Hollywood's most prestigious roles: as Scarlett O'Hara in *Gone With the Wind*, 1939, and as Blanche Dubois in *A Streetcar Named Desire*, 1951. They are both quintessentially American characters, both Southern belles, both difficult and complex parts offering formidable obstacles to success. Yet Vivien Leigh made them her own, winning two Oscars in the process. Perhaps, as is often said, people recognized a little bit of Leigh herself in the characters: Scarlett was bold, impetuous, demanding and overreaching; Blanche was faded, neurotic, self-dramatizing and very sad. Both were ultimately unsympathetic and tragically flawed, and in that verdict lies the key to Vivien Leigh's own story.

She rose to prominence in the London theatre in the late thirties, and after playing opposite Laurence Olivier in *Fire Over England* and *21 Days*, both 1937 and both for Alexander Korda, she shone as Ophelia to Olivier's Hamlet in the stage production. Her other British films included a role as Robert Taylor's leading lady in *A Yank at Oxford*, 1938. She first went to Hollywood to join Olivier, by then her lover, and it was fortuitous that preparations for *Gone With the Wind* should be in full swing — but with no-one yet chosen to play opposite Clark Gable. Legend has it that she was introduced to producer David O. Selznick as Scarlett O'Hara, and any indecision was quashed by a superb screen test. To Gable's Rhett Butler she is the perfect match: he is resourceful, exciting and roguish; she is intense, hot-tempered and highly strung. Together they are charming screen lovers, giving performances which somehow manage to rise above the fiery sunsets, cannonfire and cast of thousands.

LEFT: *Fire Over England*, 1937, with
    Laurence Olivier
OPPOSITE: publicity portrait for *Waterloo
    Bridge*, 1940.
    Photographer Laszlo Willinger

She married Olivier in 1940, high on success with both their stars shining brightly; for a short while they were the world's most brilliant couple. But although they were teamed in Korda's American costume drama, *That Hamilton Woman*, 1941, it had been decided, much to her annoyance, that her leading man in *Waterloo Bridge*, 1940, should be Robert Taylor. Her Selznick contract was by now hampering her own wishes, and it was only in the costly *Caesar and Cleopatra*, 1945, that she hit a role which corresponded to her status, if not her talents.

On screen Leigh could project a dazzling array of moods. She was alternately flirtatious and kittenish, then monstrously overbearing and vengeful, switching in the blink of an eye. The change was alarming, sometimes shocking, but always dramatically effective. If it seemed purely the technique of a skilled actress, that assumption was unfortunately undermined as rumours of serious mental illness began to reach the public ear. Although she continued acting, her battle against tuberculosis and her mental condition began to consume her energies, and her career was subsequently erratic. She died in 1967.

At her best, notably in *Gone With the Wind* and *A Streetcar Named Desire*, Leigh was utterly magnetic and quite unlike any of her competitors, with an ability to communicate a depth of feeling at which others could only hint. It is tragic that her instinctive flair for the drama of a character's self-destruction should have been converted, as with other actresses, into gripping material for a true-life showbiz spectacle.

ABOVE: *Gone With the Wind*, 1939, with Clark Gable
RIGHT: publicity portrait for *Gone With the Wind*, 1939.
Photographer Laszlo Willinger
OPPOSITE: studio portrait, 1949.
Photographer Angus McBean

THE NEO-CLASSICS

Slowly, imperceptibly, Old Hollywood began to change in the forties. *Gone With the Wind*, 1939, and *Citizen Kane*, 1941, had proved high points in the craft and artistry of film-making. Both were ambitious, audacious, pioneering attempts to create a new frontier for popular cinema. *Gone With the Wind* was a sweeping epic which mobilized the troops of producer David O. Selznick into a romantic vision of the American Civil War, the backdrop for the passionate love affair of Rhett Butler (Clark Gable) and Scarlett O'Hara (Vivien Leigh). *Citizen Kane* took advantage of advanced techniques of sound mixing, new lenses and set design so that director Orson Welles could spin a bewitching yarn of a great American newspaper tycoon in a seamless web of multiple flashbacks. Both were the dreams of tireless mavericks, utilizing the best of a settled Hollywood establishment. For many observers, they represented the peak of what had gone before, rather than the shape of things to come.

Despite the uncertainty of the Depression, and the loss of foreign markets because of the outbreak of war in Europe in 1939, Hollywood became increasingly profitable. Wartime provided easy profits from fewer movies, such was the demand for escapism and entertainment. The return of troops and the ending of hostilities made 1946 the industry's most profitable year ever, and a certain cosiness settled in the corridors of the Big Five studios: MGM, Paramount, Warners, 20th Century Fox and RKO. Although their scriptwriters, directors and even their movies were quick to respond, nobody in executive management perceived the radical social changes which were to alter American habits after the war and make the home, the family and the automobile the new nexus of the leisured classes.

So, for the time being, the 1940s saw Old Hollywood remake itself in its own image, like a sequel which didn't quite possess the magic of the original. The essential concept was *streamlining*. Attention was on refinement, variation and detail of old formulae, and, like revamped automobiles, stars were stripped down, remodelled, and scaled down ready for mass production. Into Garbo's roles stepped both Ingrid Bergman and Hedy Lamarr, the latter herself replaced by Yvonne De Carlo as the formula slowly began to diminish in strength. Lana Turner became a forties version of Harlow, clad this time in a sweater rather than a satin dress. From the era of glamour shots, with MGM's Adrian outstyling the Parisian *haute-couturiers*, the studios introduced that of pin-ups of different varieties of beefcake and cheesecake.

The favourite GI pin-ups were Betty Grable, Hedy Lamarr, Ann Sheridan ('the Oomph Girl'), Rita Hayworth, Dorothy Lamour, Veronica Lake and Lana Turner. As they posed in their swimsuits, sweaters and sarongs, it seemed their wartime male audience could be relied upon to long insatiably for these all-American girls. Their glamour was never as exotic, as perverse or as splendid as that of the thirties Dietrich; instead, their approachability and availability were emphasized. Exoticism was reserved for the Latin-American spitfire, of which Maria Montez and Carmen Miranda were camp varieties, and the dark beauty of Ava Gardner a rather more sensual one.

Combat movies like *Thirty Seconds Over Tokyo*, 1944, and *Objective Burma!*, 1945, had an obvious masculine bias, whereas *Casablanca* and *Mrs Miniver*, both 1942, and *The Best Years of Our Lives*, 1946, were solid examples of mainstream dramas that combined war interest with strong roles for leading ladies like Ingrid Bergman, Greer Garson and Myrna Loy. But the most exciting development was to one side of the mainstream, in the *film noir*. From the beginning of the

1940s a new mood was recognizable in a string of usually low-budget thrillers, starting with *The Maltese Falcon*, 1941, and *This Gun for Hire*, 1942. They featured cynical, disillusioned heroes in dingy, urban, night-time settings, and the mood was typically sombre and bleak. Into this *film noir* atmosphere of corruption and pessimism stepped a new kind of leading lady, a variation on the romantic *femme fatale* from European literature and painting of the late nineteenth century. She was almost always bewitchingly glamorous, slow to befriend and swift to betray, a haunting and often malevolently dangerous vision which could lure a man to his doom, or bring him to despair. Barbara Stanwyck in *Double Indemnity*, 1944, Gene Tierney in *Laura*, 1944, Veronica Lake in *This Gun for Hire*, and *The Glass Key*, both 1942, Lana Turner in *Johnny Eager*, 1941, and *The Postman Always Rings Twice*, 1946, Lauren Bacall in *To Have and Have Not*, 1944, and, more strictly, in *The Big Sleep*, 1946, Rita Hayworth in *Gilda*, 1946, and *The Lady from Shanghai*, 1947, all embodied this persona of a calculating heroine who could outwit her leading man and possibly trick him into sudden death. Traditionally the figure of the *femme fatale* is seen as an object of male fantasies, a creation of his paranoid fears and sexual insecurity. Certainly the new breed of leading men seemed generally morose, masochistic and misogynistic, in the form of Glenn Ford, Dana Andrews and Victor Mature. Only John Garfield's and Humphrey Bogart's sense of alienation was positive rather than self-destructive, while the likes of Farley Granger and Van Johnson seemed bland, and Dan Duryea and Van Heflin pathetically tough.

They were a long way from the charm of Cary Grant, the rock-like presence of Gregory Peck, the stiff upper lip of David Niven or the gentlemanly sneer of James Mason, which all featured so heavily later in the forties. For a while it appeared that the wartime stereotype of the strong male had been undermined and mocked. Women like Hayworth, Gardner and Turner – the Rita-Ava-Lana triumvirate – combined traditionally male strengths with a hard, glamorous mystique of their own. They were equally at home in broad-shouldered suits or silk and lamé nightgowns, and could be independent, determined and resolute without their men. This sense of the strong female who had usurped the traditional role of the man derived at least in part from the wartime experience of women, who had for a time formed America's workforce; but it had the added twist of making them the icons *par excellence* for male homosexual culture after the war was over.

The use of real urban locations in *film noir* also spilled over into a new realism, seen in *The House on 92nd Street*, 1945, and *Naked City*, 1948, for example, and this combined with a different tradition in Italian neo-realist films such as Rossellini's *Roma Città aperta*, 1945. Nevertheless, the concentration on colourful, escapist fantasy continued in the form of Esther Williams' Technicolor water-sports, the Crosby-Hope-Lamour *Road* series, anything featuring Carmen Miranda or Maria Montez, and most notably in MGM's support for the musicals of Gene Kelly, Vincente Minnelli and Arthur Freed, in which Judy Garland and Cyd Charisse led the field. By the end of the decade even Warner Brothers went over to colour and took on Doris Day for *Romance On the High Seas*, 1948, although some stars, like Joan Crawford and Claudette Colbert, consistently avoided colour movies.

The end of the 1940s saw Old Hollywood finally on the wane. *Sunset Boulevard*, 1950, was its wittiest epitaph, and *All About Eve*, 1950, was a crystallization of the lessons that one generation had learnt by imitating the techniques and tricks of a previous one. There was nothing more to glean. The revival of the French and Italian film industries after the Liberation caused a fresh sense of opportunity and enthusiasm to join with older traditions of cinematic excellence in those countries; and the films of Carné, Becker, Melville, Autant-Lara, Duvivier and Allégret in France, and Rossellini, Visconti, De Santis, De Sica and later Fellini in Italy were to create a sensation.

In 1948 two killer blows were dealt to the Hollywood business, both self-inflicted. The rapacity and greed of the Big Five studios had caused the US government to bring an anti-Trust suit against their monopolistic control of the film industry, and a ruling demanded that they strip themselves of the chains of cinemas upon which their stranglehold over the industry was based. In addition, Senator Joe McCarthy's House Of Un-American Activities Committee began to investigate allegedly pro-Communist sympathizers in Hollywood, and the eagerness of the studio bosses to co-operate produced a blacklist that included some of their most talented artists and performers, as well as a stifling atmosphere of suspicion and fear. When European governments, including Britain, began to impose penalties on American firms withdrawing funds from their countries, a new policy was started to produce films domestically in Britain, Italy, France and Spain. A pattern was developing from the ruins of Old Hollywood, and no doubt there were many who were glad of it.

BARBARA STANWYCK

For three decades Barbara Stanwyck was one of Hollywood's most reliable leading ladies, with an enviable range and longevity. She starred opposite a young Clark Gable in the early thirties; and she was still dynamite, literally, in Sam Fuller's phallic Western, *Forty Guns*, 1957. Yet her relatively low status today is a puzzle. She vied with Joan Crawford and Bette Davis as an interpreter of roles for strong women, outshining Crawford's talent for melodrama without resorting to camp, and well able to match Davis quip for quip

OPPOSITE: studio portrait, 1939.
          Photographer Eugene Robert Richee
LEFT: publicity portrait for *Ball of Fire*, 1941, with
          Gary Cooper.
          Photographer George Hurrell
BELOW: *Double Indemnity*, 1944, with
          Fred MacMurray and Tom Powers

in her acid-flavoured drawl. Even in terms of temperament she was beyond reproach. But for some reason her image lacks the grandeur of either Davis' or Crawford's. Why?

A glance at three performances which won her Oscar nominations gives some idea. In *Double Indemnity*, 1944, she defines the bewitching *femme fatale* of the rest of the decade in a devastating portrayal of a middle-class Medusa involved in murder. Dressed and bobbed like some blonde voodoo doll, she fixes accomplice Fred MacMurray with a cute smile – but she can turn wicked with the twitch of an eyebrow. Only seven years before Stanwyck had tugged at the heart-strings as a long-suffering mother in *Stella Dallas*, 1937; and in between she was the wisecracking singer Sugarpuss O'Shea who charmed a bumbling professor (Gary Cooper) in the vintage screwball comedy *Ball of Fire*, 1941. In all three Stanwyck avoids that triumph of personality over part that gave her rivals such long-lived distinction. From the fresh-faced Yankee heroine in love with a Chinese warlord in *The Bitter Tea of General Yen*, 1932, to the hard-boiled matriarch opposite Ronald Reagan in *Cattle Queen of Montana*, 1954, Stanwyck could play them all. With her fluid and suggestive looks she could act the tough-hearted thirties gold digger, yet could project an open-eyed enthusiasm as convincingly as a soured spinster's revenge.

Stanwyck's performance in *Double Indemnity* has rarely been bettered; but in the *film noir* cycle of *The Two Mrs Carrolls*, 1946, *Sorry, Wrong Number*, 1948 (which brought another Oscar nomination), and *The File On Thelma Jordan*, 1949, she gave three more performances which would each suffice as the high point of any one actress' career.

ABOVE: studio portrait, c. 1945.
Photographer Bert Six
RIGHT: *The Other Love*, 1947, with David Niven
OPPOSITE: studio portrait, 1937.
Photographer Robert W. Coburn

GENE TIERNEY

It is poetic justice that one of Gene Tierney's best roles was as a painting that bewitches detective Dana Andrews in *Laura*, 1944, Otto Preminger's *film noir* mystery. For she was so obviously at her best as a dreamy *femme fatale* that to bring her into dull reality seemed to defeat the object of the exercise.

She came from a wealthy New York family, and progressed from Broadway to 20th Century Fox. There she was given a strong role in Fritz Lang's *The Return of Jesse James*, 1940, the lead in the Western, *Belle Starr*, 1941, and a good part opposite Don Ameche in Lubitsch's *Heaven Can Wait*, 1943. She became perversely typecast at this time as an all-purpose oriental, the result of confusing her feline charms with eastern-style promise; but despite *Shanghai Gesture* and *Son of Fury*, both 1941, her strongest roles were American through and through. Her most popular movie was *Leave Her to Heaven*, 1945, directed by the melodrama king John M. Stahl. Tierney received an Oscar nomination for her paranoid portrait of a woman who steals her sister's lover and kills her unborn baby, among many other sins. She was unnervingly perfect in a world where passions lead to obsession and disaster. A success as a disturbed beauty in Preminger's *Whirlpool*, 1949, meant she came to be associated with characters driven by torment, on the verge of losing control. As one of the first actresses to exploit the post-war fascination with neurosis, it is ironic that her own nervous breakdown in the early 1950s led to her semi-retirement from the screen.

LEFT: publicity portrait for *The Shanghai Gesture*, 1941

If Joan Fontaine, the younger sister of Olivia De Havilland, had settled down with first husband Brian Aherne in 1940 after an inauspicious series of leading roles at RKO, those two Hitchcock masterpieces *Rebecca*, 1940, and *Suspicion*, 1941, and Max Ophüls' dreamlike *Letter From an Unknown Woman*, 1948, might all have been lesser works. She was quieter than her sister, but more subtly intense; and for the part of the second Mrs de Winter, wife to Laurence Olivier, in *Rebecca*, Hitchcock saw she had a unique advantage over other candidates like Vivien Leigh or Anne Baxter. 'I could see her potential for restrained acting and I felt she could play the character in a quiet, shy manner,' he recalled. She manages to portray a brooding anxiety and terror that builds into a climax as taut as a whiplash; she was nominated for an Oscar for the performance, and the film won Best Picture. The same qualities were central in *Suspicion*, when Fontaine is driven to the verge of madness by fears that her husband Cary Grant is a murderer; this time she won the Oscar, triumphing over her sister in the process, and establishing a wider emotional range for female characters. Ophüls' *Letter From an Unknown Woman* is a variation on that theme, a Viennese whirl through the past and present of a love affair that surges into passionate life through Fontaine's memory. Fontaine's career coincided with Hollywood's obsession with psychoanalysis, and with characters awash in a sea of neurosis; her calm features remained the perfect counterpoint to the angst that lurked beneath the surface.

RIGHT: studio portrait, c. 1940

IDA LUPINO

Ida Lupino was an ideal heroine in several Warner Bros. action yarns, and one who nowadays should be more in vogue; for she sums up that early forties sense of disillusionment, weary toughness and preparedness for heart-ache. Moody and beautiful, but without needing to rely on her looks, she rose above weak material with staggering ease. Her obvious intelligence found expression in her later work as scriptwriter, director and producer from the fifties onwards.

Born in London, the daughter of acrobat–comedian Stanley Lupino, Lupino made a prolonged detour through such oddball Hollywood productions as the surrealist *Peter Ibbetson*, 1935, Jack Benny's *Artists and Models*, 1937, and *The Adventures of Sherlock Holmes*, 1939, before finding her feet with a seven-year contract at Warners just as their tough-guy gangster cycle was coming to a close. There she sparked flirtatiously opposite George Raft and Bogart in *They Drive by Night*, 1940; but she came into her own with a strong role in Raoul Walsh's follow-up, *High Sierra*, 1941, as Marie Garson, a taxi dancer bruised and on the rebound, who sides with the doomed outlaw Roy Earle (Bogart) against the law, the cops, and the sad world of 'twerps, soda jerkers and jitterbugs'. It set her up for major roles in *The Sea Wolf*, *Out of the Fog*, both 1941, *Moontide*, 1942, opposite Jean Gabin, and as a hard-driving career girl in *The Hard Way*, 1943, in an award-winning performance. She had strong competition at Warners from Bette Davis, Ann Sheridan and Joan Crawford, but seemed to hint at a niche for herself as a female Bogart that she never quite found on screen.

LEFT: publicity portrait for *The Man I Love*, 1947.
    Photographer Bert Six
OPPOSITE: studio portrait, 1941.
    Photographer Scotty Welbourne

VERONICA LAKE

Veronica Lake was pure *film noir* vamp, a real man-eater. Opposite co-star Alan Ladd it seemed as though she could quite happily finish off the little squirt with one quick gulp. In their three hits together – *This Gun for Hire, The Glass Key*, both 1942, and *The Blue Dahlia*, 1946 – male insecurity was never more evident, as Ladd put on trenchcoat and hat, and sported a gun as much in self-defence as to assert himself as a hero of the urban streets. Although Ladd and Lake had got there first, the Bogart and Bacall partnership did at least have an element of tension; if Lake had whistled at Ladd, you feel she could have blown him away.

Lake was the daughter of a German–Danish seaman, her striking looks accentuated by the veil of her blonde peek-a-boo hairstyle. It proved so popular with women in the USA's wartime factories that the government made an official request to Paramount for Lake to crop it – to prevent industrial accidents. Her deep voice rounded off a supreme wartime fantasy that found form in her exaggeratedly glamorous persona. Although it is in her films with Ladd that she is best remembered, she was possibly better used in a couple of superb comedies, Preston Sturges' *Sullivan's Travels*, 1941, and Rene Clair's *I Married a Witch*, 1942, in which her sophisticated image is treated more light-heartedly. But once deprived of her distinctive hairstyle, Lake never really recovered her momentum. She filed for bankruptcy in the early fifties; thus her career waxed and waned within a single decade.

LEFT: studio portrait, 1940.
Photographer Eugene Robert Richee

OPPOSITE: studio portrait, 1945.
Photographer Ernest A. Bachrach

In Ingrid Bergman's career there are more than superficial resemblances to the fate of her Swedish compatriot, Greta Garbo. There are obvious similarities in their acting styles, especially when viewed from the distant perspective of a Californian executive's armchair; but there are less happy comparisons in the way both were built up and applauded, only to disappear when they 'disobeyed' a particular strand of Hollywood's code of behaviour. Both became Queens of Hollywood, yet accepted exile at the height of their fame.

Bergman was a leading actress in Sweden when her film *Intermezzo*,

RIGHT: *Gaslight*, 1944, with Charles Boyer
BELOW: *En Enda Natt*, 1939

1936, came to the attention of producer David O. Selznick. At great expense he imported her to Hollywood, where he promoted her as a great natural beauty who, like some seedling plucked from a Scandinavian forest, needed no make-up to be fully appreciated. Her Hollywood debut was in a remake of *Intermezzo*, co-starring Leslie Howard and released in 1939. After that her career zigzagged, for she was personally contracted to Selznick and he was taking a break from movie-making. Loaned out to various studios she played diverse roles, from a tarty barmaid in *Dr Jekyll and Mr Hyde*, 1941, to a Hedy Lamarr

LEFT: *Casablanca*, 1942, with Humphrey Bogart
BELOW: *Spellbound*, 1945

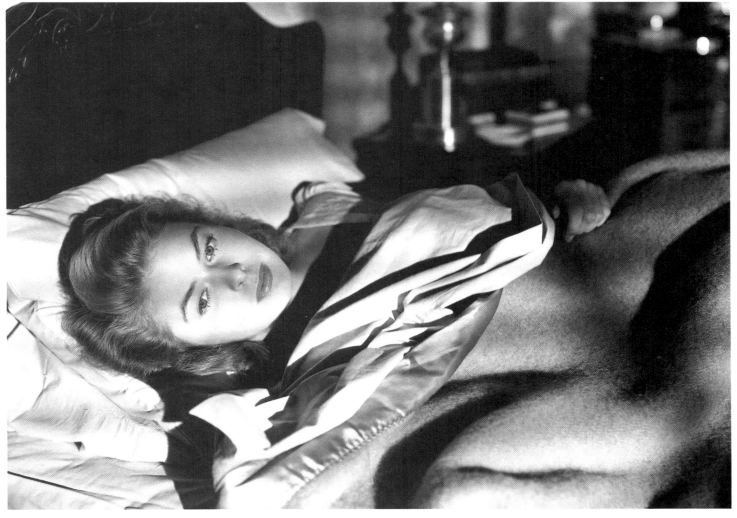

121

replacement opposite Bogart in *Casablanca*, 1942, in which she is torn between love for her old flame Rick and loyalty to her husband. In a potentially banal setting, she proved her talent for the understatement of intense emotion. Selznick persuaded Hemingway to endorse her as the lead in *For Whom the Bell Tolls*, 1943; and she really came into her own with *Gaslight*, 1944, for which she won an Oscar for her interpretation of a wife slowly going insane under the tormenting of her husband, played by Charles Boyer.

From then on, she seemed to do little wrong, especially for Hitchcock in *Spellbound*, 1945, with Gregory Peck, and in *Notorious*, 1946, opposite Cary Grant and Claude Rains, her last films under contract to Selznick. In *Notorious* she played a spy engaged in undercover work, apparently cast off by Grant in a callous denial of their love, and in Hitchcock's erotically long, lingering shots Bergman is magnetic. *The Bells of St Mary's*, 1945, with Bing Crosby, didn't quite hit the same standard, although it was her biggest box office success to date and earned her an Oscar nomination. Nothing, it seemed, could displace her as the nation's top dramatic star.

Except a scandal. After *Joan of Arc*, 1948, she left Hollywood for Italy, where she fell in love with movie director Roberto Rossellini and bore his child out of wedlock (they married in 1950). Vilified, denounced and virtually blacklisted by the American press for her sins, her powerful performances in his *Stromboli*, 1949, *Europa '51*, 1951, and *Viaggio in Italia*, 1953, were almost ignored in the USA. After Hollywood's careful artifice, these films were raw and compellingly rough, with plots more angst-laden and bleak than her usual happy endings. Nothing detracted from the strength of her emotions, and her charisma shone through the

LEFT: *For Whom the Bell Tolls*, 1943, with
　　　Gary Cooper
OPPOSITE: publicity portrait for *Notorious*, 1946,
　　　with Cary Grant.
　　　Photographer Ernest A. Bachrach

films' often sketchy characterizations.

It was said that American audiences only loved her when she was playing a *good* woman. However incredible this puritanism may seem for the supposedly rocking 'n' rolling fifties, Bergman was on the receiving end of it for many years. She was only publicly forgiven with an Oscar for her part in the American production, *Anastasia*, 1956, in which she played the pretender to the Tsar's throne. This and another noble weepie, *The Inn of the Sixth Happiness*, 1958, were saturated with suffering in adversity; and they carried a masochistic undertow to them which tilted her performances towards mawkish sentiment. In that same year her marriage to Rossellini was dissolved, and she later married a Swedish stage producer.

Like Garbo, Bergman possessed the ability to suggest great depth of emotion without histrionics; and it is that ability which so many American actresses have lacked. She knew the secret of hinting at inner terror without resorting to outward babble, and of projecting that uncannily clearly on screen. But unlike Garbo, she seemed devoid of a lasting independence from men: she could suffer in silence, but always seemed to believe that her characters' happiness depended ultimately on being one half of a partnership. This sense possibly made her movies more interesting dramas, but perhaps detracted from her eventual stature as a star; for in that slight weakness, she compromised her mythical status and descended to the all-too-recognizable reality that most of us inhabit.

ABOVE: publicity portrait for *Saratoga Trunk*, 1945.
Photographer Scotty Welbourne
RIGHT: *Stromboli*, 1949

In our imagination Michèle Morgan remains forever shrouded in the mists of Marcel Carné's *Quai des brumes*, 1938, a petite figure dressed in trench-coat and beret and just visible behind a foggy window with lover Jean Gabin. She was only eighteen years old, a discovery of French director Marc Allégret, but her phenomenal pres-ence as the mysterious, knowing girl who enjoys a tragically brief affair with Gabin remained with her for the rest of her life. Its success brought her to Hollywood, where she narrowly mis-sed what would become an equally myth-laden role opposite Bogart in *Casablanca*, 1942. She did, however, get the leading part in *Passage to Marseille*, 1943, with Bogart, but she never quite showed her true potential, and was always disappointed with the roles Hollywood found for her. Her trenchcoat and beret suited her well, seemingly symbols of a fleeting and furtive romance with unknown future. One remembers her strong features disappearing into the mist, maybe never to be seen again. . . .

After the war, when she returned to Paris, she quickly established herself as one of France's leading actresses. She won the Best Actress award at Cannes in 1946 for her role in *La Symphonie pastorale*, in which she plays the blind girl who falls in love with a priest. She consolidated her position throughout the fifties. But directors seemed to require little of her other than a regal tranquillity; and perhaps it was boredom which caused her to re-tire in 1968, to spend more time in the fashion industry. She remains a legendary figure for French filmgoers, enjoying popularity on a par with Bardot, Deneuve or Moreau.

RIGHT: studio portrait, 1940.
　　Photographer Ernest A. Bachrach

SIMONE SIMON

In her French movies, Simone Simon's petite face and feline expression were used as symbols of natural beauty, whether with young lover Jean-Pierre Aumont in *Le Lac aux dames*, 1934, or later in Jean Renoir's *La Bête humaine*, 1938. But in America she became famous for the opposite. Those same features were used as material for dreams and horror; although she still looked pretty, innocent and very French, the interpretation of her beauty was wildly different.

Simon had two attempts at making a successful Hollywood career. In 1936 she had gone there to work for 20th Century Fox, but dissatisfaction with her employers brought her back to France within two years. *La Bête humaine* prompted an invitation to return and it was during this second spell – which lasted until the end of World War Two – that she made that classic of horror movies, *Cat People*, 1942.

In that film Simon plays the central role, caught in the web of a plot which is as effective as it is unlikely. She is a young girl haunted by sexual fears, who comes to believe she is descended from an ancient race of cat-worshippers. In director Jacques Tourneur's treatment her inner psychological torment is conveyed with a dreamlike play of light and dark-ness on her face in a gripping series of set-pieces; shadowy figures of giant cats suggest a secret, hidden and unnatural life. She projects a curious mix of contrasting emotions which Simon's character both fears and pities; she is not a straightforward *femme fatale*, for she is herself a victim of the unconscious fears that engulf her. Simon's appearance is pure, unsullied and vulnerable; forty years later when Nastassja Kinski played the same part in a remake, the character became both corrupt and corrupting.

ABOVE: publicity portrait for *Cat People*, 1942. Photographer Ernest A. Bachrach

For over three decades Danielle Darrieux was one of France's leading stars, a perennial favourite and a more adaptable rival to Michèle Morgan. She covered almost every genre from comedy to adventure, high drama to musicals, modern to classical, in a career that began at the age of fourteen when her mother pushed her to audition for *Le Bal*, 1932. Darrieux achieved international fame when she played Maria Vetsera opposite Charles Boyer's Prince Rudolph in *Mayerling*, 1936, a baroque romantic tragedy of suicide in the Hapsburg court. Hollywood then enticed her over the Atlantic to play in *The Rage of Paris*, 1938, memorably promoting her with the slogan 'Fifty million Frenchmen can't be wrong!' The studio could not overcome her reluctance to stay in California, however, even though they tried to enforce what they saw as a legal obligation on her to do so; Darrieux's career was to be truly international. After the war, mostly spent in occupied Paris, she made three films with director Max Ophüls, whose complex constructions and elaborate camerawork framed Darrieux to best advantage. She played opposite Daniel Gelin and Fernand Gravey in *La Ronde*, 1950, and then as a Maupassant heroine – a prostitute – loved by Jean Gabin in the central story of *Le Plaisir*, 1951. Yet strongest of all was her performance in the title role of *Madame de . . .*, 1953, in which a pair of pawned ear-rings spins an ironic web around the trio of fashionable lovers. Despite her many modern incarnations on stage and screen during the fifties and sixties, she is best remembered for this image, a poised and sophisticated woman in satin ballgown, opposite lover Vittorio De Sica and husband Charles Boyer.

RIGHT: publicity portrait for *Ruy Blas*, 1948.
Photographer Raymond Voinquel

ARLETTY

As the central romantic figure of Marcel Carné's epic *Les Enfants du paradis*, 1944, Arletty occupies a similar role in French lore to Scarlett O'Hara in America: a woman desired by all men, fickle and impulsive, deeply passionate yet doomed to unhappiness. Her role as Garance, the courtesan, is the pivot around which this sprawling, magnificent movie turns, as she is pursued by four lovers – Jean-Louis Barrault, Pierre Brasseur, Louis Salou and Marcel Herrand. She sustains the film without swamping it, a performance of precisely judged nuances that has grown in stature even after its huge contemporary success.

Arletty (born Léonie Bathiat) had already appeared in other classics, among them Carné's *Le Jour se lève*, 1939, and *Les Visiteurs du soir*, 1942, in which she is a world-weary heroine in a haunting landscape that captured the uncertainty of these years. She was in her forties by then and reaching the peak of a long career spent until 1931 in the music hall and on stage. The aura of an older woman is accentuated by the complete assurance which she brings to all her performances. She was able, for instance, to dominate the screen version of Jean-Paul Sartre's *Huis clos*, 1954, as a tormenting lesbian, seemingly terrifying her fellow actors. Overall, she has no match in the American cinema as an actress, since her persona is mature and adult, and she is expert at portraying sombre emotions and passions unmistakably born out of real-life experience. After the liberation of Paris she was briefly jailed for collaboration with the Germans because of a love affair with a Nazi officer, and she has done very little on stage or screen since the early sixties.

OPPOSITE: *Les Visiteurs du soir*, 1942
ABOVE: *Les Enfants du paradis*, 1944, with Jean-Louis Barrault
LEFT: *Le Jour se lève*, 1939

MAUREEN O'HARA

There used to be a corner of Hollywood's imagination that was forever Ireland, a lush Eden of distant dreams and harsh, rural realities. Films like *How Green Was My Valley*, 1941, *Rio Grande*, 1950, *The Quiet Man*, 1952, or *The Long Gray Line*, 1955, all directed by John Ford, may have been set in Wales or Texas, but at their heart was always Maureen O'Hara, the Dublin girl whose flaming red hair and green eyes made her 'Queen of Technicolor'.

She had been noticed by Charles Laughton in Hitchcock's British production of *Jamaica Inn*, 1939, and he took her to Hollywood to play the female lead to his Quasimodo in *The Hunchback of Notre Dame*, 1939. But it was her portrayal of a daughter of a Welsh mining family in *How Green Was My Valley* that set the tone for her best roles in the future. She was strongest as a woman in an all-male society, an arbiter of passions and loyalties that forced order on a group. She played a stubborn, determined character more often than not, with a fiery temper easily sparked by some male insensitivity. No male could have been more insensitive than John Wayne, against whom she repeatedly railed, shouted, cursed and cajoled — before melting into his arms. *The Quiet Man*, for example, is both horribly sentimental and rousingly passionate about Wayne and O'Hara's romance; she is the headstrong village girl, who stands by while her suitors come to blows for her attention, and secretly wills her favourite to victory. By the time that movie was made, O'Hara was well on her way to establishing herself as a spirited star of the Western, and that genre sustained her throughout the fifties and sixties. She played opposite Wayne in the Western, *Big Jake*, 1971, but by then their brand of romance had had its day.

LEFT: *The Quiet Man*, 1952, with John Wayne

Ann Sheridan was a teacher who turned into a glamour queen. She was the 'Oomph Girl', one of that unholy trinity (with Betty Grable and Rita Hayworth) who sent GI pulses racing. Svelte, pouting, with a look just this side of contemptuous, she had the archetypal glamour-girl career — winning a beauty contest, playing bit parts for Paramount, and graduating to become the 'Oomph Girl' at Warners three years later; by the time producers discovered she really could act after all, she was well into her thirties and on her way out at the box office.

As a Warners contract player, Sheridan stood her ground with stars like Cagney in *Angels With Dirty Faces*, 1938, *Torrid Zone*, 1940, and *City for Conquest*, 1940, snapping back in similar machine-gun bursts to his own. She was just as self-assured opposite Bogart and George Raft in *They Drive by Night*, 1941, for which she received equal top billing. She excelled at that bemused, dismissive look which caused her strutting male stars to take a deep breath, grind their teeth, and let forth a kind of whimpering growl.

She was a big hit in an emotionally charged drama, *Kings Row*, 1942, in which Ronald Reagan loses his legs, but she preferred her work in comedies. *I Was a Male War Bride*, 1949, a madcap Hawksian fable featuring Cary Grant in drag, was her best effort. And she pulled off a late surprise as the heroine of *Take Me to Town*, 1953, an unlikely musical by Douglas Sirk, in which she played a vaudevillian stepmother. She had been typecast too strongly, however, to weather a complete change of image, and she was left to smoulder in the wartime generation's memories on television during the rest of the fifties.

ABOVE: studio portrait, c. 1940.
Photographer Scotty Welbourne

LANA TURNER

In her early career Lana Turner was billed variously, as the successor to Harlow, or perhaps Crawford; they said she would inherit the type of roles made famous by Loy or Colbert; or she was the forces' favourite pin-up, 'The Sweater Girl'. It was some time before this pneumatic blonde came into her own as the very epitome of a tinseltown movie star. Her plastic features and cantilevered frame could have been immaculately conceived in the famous Hollywood drugstore where she was by legend discovered; for Turner was the triumph of plucked-eyebrow-artifice over reality.

Turner began in bit-parts as a favourite of director Mervyn LeRoy, but soon graduated after *Dancing Co-Ed*, 1939, to bigger parts. MGM tried her out opposite their top male leads in *Dr*

Jekyll and Mr Hyde, 1941, with Spencer Tracy, in *Honky Tonk*, 1942, with Clark Gable, and in an early attempt at *film noir* opposite Robert Taylor, *Johnny Eager*, 1942. But her lack of training could not be disguised: every slight expression of grief seemed to swell to fever pitch, every smile of joy just missed bringing tears to her eyes. Only when she landed the part of the scheming wife Cora in Tay Garnett's *The Postman Always Rings Twice*, 1946, did she begin to show her peculiar genius. Her screen lover John Garfield was her polar opposite: ruggedly sincere, unashamedly working class, naturally simple. When she rolls her lipstick over towards him in the opening scene, his face registers surprise at this invitation to the world her character represents: a world of

money-lust, shameful passion, petty aspirations, a world which will shortly engulf them both.

There followed a run of hit movies, competition at MGM with Elizabeth Taylor and Ava Gardner, and then a breakthrough with a lead part in Vincente Minnelli's *The Bad and the Beautiful*, 1952, a seamy melodrama of Hollywood life in which Turner plays an ambitious, egotistical star-monster. She was very good at it. Her leading part in *Peyton Place*, 1958, came along after she had been dropped by MGM, but it brought her an Oscar nomination for her role as a suburban mother who

ABOVE: studio portrait, c. 1938.
Photographer Laszlo Willinger
OPPOSITE: studio portrait, 1942.
Photographer Eric Carpenter

doesn't understand her daughter.

Some called her performance in the witness stand that same year her best ever: she was defending her daughter who had killed Turner's lover, gangster Johnny Stompanato, with a bread-knife. The case brought revelations of torrid sex secrets, making front-page news for months, and it prompted producer Ross Hunter to select her for Douglas Sirk's remake of *Imitation of Life*, 1958, in which she plays an ambitious star whose adopted half-caste daughter goes off the rails. She was highly convincing as the manipulative

RIGHT: *The Postman Always Rings Twice*, 1946, with John Garfield
BELOW: publicity portrait for *The Rains of Ranchipur*, 1955, with Richard Burton

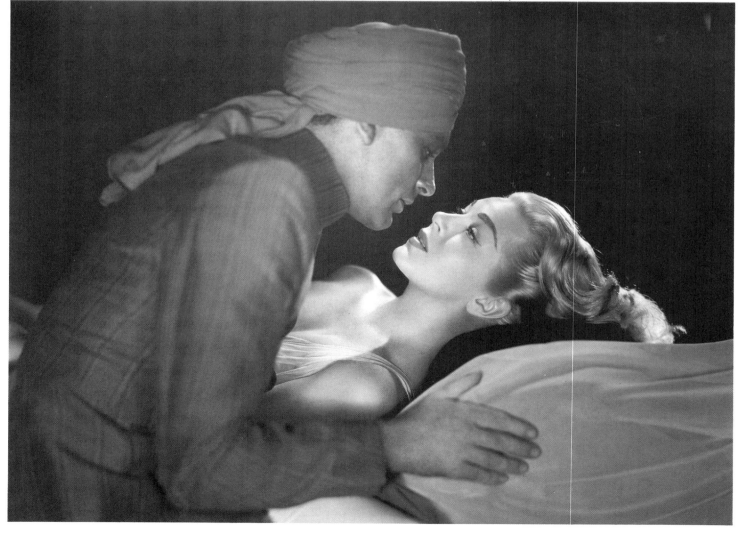

career woman whose life of material comfort conceals a tawdry and un-giving emotional life. For some it is merely cheap melodrama; but as Turner's own life had shown, it was that potent sense of disaster about to emerge from the celluloid American dream that made her performance so tearfully moving. It was all so fitting for a poor small-time girl who had been shot to stardom, whose real-life romances and seven marriages included a bandleader, a gangster, a playboy-millionaire, an actor and one ex-Tarzan, Lex Barker.

LEFT: off set *Diane*, 1955
BELOW: *Johnny Eager*, 1942, with Robert Taylor

LAUREN BACALL

When Lauren Bacall instructed Bogart on how to whistle in her film debut, *To Have and Have Not*, 1944, something novel was happening. For over and above her husky voice, slinky figure and beautifully alert face, Bacall possessed an attitude that was definably new. It was as if this wisecracking nineteen-year-old had taken something from the Bogart mould and fashioned it for herself. Bacall looked, sounded, acted as if she belonged to no-one. It was a striking pose. Even Bogart looks faintly bemused as he purses his lips and lets out the most admiring whistle you'll ever hear.

Born in New York City, Bacall had been working as a model there until Howard Hawks' wife spotted her picture on the cover of 'Harper's Bazaar'. With no acting experience, she was coached intensively into her first performance. Yet in *To Have and Have Not* and *The Big Sleep*, 1946, Bogart and Bacall established a novel rapport of mutual self-respect which went against the grain of *film noir* relationships. Ladd and Lake were mere high-gloss figments of the imagination in comparison, while the William Powell–Myrna Loy partnership seemed like a relic of thirties conventionality. When Bogart and Bacall married in 1945, they seemed like a prototype for the perfect post-war couple: he was a growling, cynical optimist who'd seen it all; she was youthful but already world-weary, and wiser than her years.

Through *Dark Passage*, 1947, and *Key Largo*, 1948, they continued and developed that relationship. Bacall began to go her own way on screen from the early fifties, and took pride in refusing roles she considered unsuitable; Warners punished her several times by suspension. In *How to Marry a Millionaire*, 1953, she was a memorable gold digger opposite Marilyn Monroe and Betty Grable, and she

OPPOSITE: studio portrait, 1946.
Photographer Scotty Welbourne
RIGHT: publicity portrait for *The Big Sleep*, 1946, with Humphrey Bogart.
Photographer John Engstead

took strong roles in *The Cobweb*, 1955, and *Written on the Wind*, 1956; but in general she seemed less than interested in most of her screen characters. Bogart died of cancer in 1957, and Bacall later married (and divorced) Jason Robards Jr.

None of Bacall's roles of the fifties seemed to fulfil her initial promise. The world was by then apparently made of plush, upholstered heroines asked only to giggle and get on with wearing out their consumer luxuries. Bacall's bleak, generous features stood out handsomely, but she never made the most of her uniqueness.

RIGHT: studio portrait, 1944.
Photographer Henry Waxman
BELOW: *Confidential Agent*, 1945, with
Charles Boyer

Never let it be said that Jennifer Jones was unadaptable. She had many of Hollywood's strongest roles in the forties, the most memorable of which went together like oil and water. She could be convincing as the young peasant girl from Lourdes who becomes a saint in *The Song of Bernadette*, 1943, and as the sexy half-breed who splits up brothers Joseph Cotten and Gregory Peck in *Duel in the Sun*, 1946. At her best in the latter, she was powerfully sensual; and her Oscar for Bernadette made her an unfading example of Hollywood piety. She was a discovery of the producer David O. Selznick, and his wife from 1949, and her career was a visible tribute to his penchant for creating characters as heroically extreme as Scarlett O'Hara.

Selznick signed her up in 1940, and over the next twenty years directed all his energies into finding suitable roles for her. Jones proved expert at wartime romance opposite real-life husband Robert Walker in *Since You Went Away*, 1944, but *Duel in the Sun*, with its baroque passions and nickname 'Lust in the Dust', perhaps allowed her capacity for subtlety to be forgotten. She was certainly better in the relatively unpretentious melodrama *Ruby Gentry*, 1953, than in Minnelli's *Madame Bovary*, 1949, in which she played the lead. After idiosyncrasies like *Beat the Devil*, 1954, and a disaster in Europe called *Stazione Termini*, 1952, she returned to form with an Oscar nomination for *Love is a Many-Splendored Thing*, 1955. Her list of credits in such prestige productions as *A Farewell to Arms*, 1957, impersonating Norma Shearer in a remake of *The Barretts of Wimpole Street*, 1957, and the weak *Tender is the Night*, 1962, confirm the suspicion that, like Shearer, she is to be regarded as a species of Hollywood royalty to whom critical standards are hardly applicable. Her career virtually ended after Selznick's death in 1965.

RIGHT: publicity portrait for *Duel in the Sun*, 1946.
Photographer Al St. Hilaire

SUSAN HAYWARD

A discovery from the cover of 'The Saturday Evening Post', Susan Hayward was a red-haired twenty-one-year-old when she tested for Scarlett O'Hara in *Gone With the Wind*. She spent the rest of her career building up to an epic intensity of performance that would have filled even that blockbuster, with some to spare. Whether her style is a glamorized version of the Method, or just plain overacting, she could always be depended upon to give her all.

After coasting through second-fiddle parts at Warners, and for Paramount in the forties, she gradually began to pick up good notices and won her first Oscar nomination for Universal's *Smash-Up: The Story of a Woman*, 1947, in which she plays a singer who hits the booze. It was only after another five years of playing in all manner of films that she at last hit her form as a crippled singer in *With a Song in My Heart*, 1952. The film restates many of the themes of *Smash-Up*, themes that were to touch most nerves for her; *I'll Cry Tomorrow*, 1956, combined them all. Hayward plays Lillian Roth, a real-life singer fighting against the bottle, travelling to hell and back in time to be saved. If Hayward's arc was interrupted by nonsense like *The Conqueror*, 1956, with John Wayne and *Untamed*, 1955, with Tyrone Power, her Oscar-winning performance in *I Want to Live!*, 1958, summed up her hysterical potential with a part as a jailed prostitute on her way to the gas chamber. She gave high-octane emotion, she was a real flamethrower that left audiences bruised, battered and scarred; yet they still loved her. Rumours that she was wanted for *Cleopatra*, 1963, proved unfounded, and she gave her last memorable performance in *Valley of the Dolls* in 1967 – but in that movie her overblown style skidded dangerously near trash. She died of a brain tumour, aged fifty-six.

LEFT: studio portrait, 1939.
Photographer Eugene Robert Richee

On one of the posters for *Gilda*, 1946, Rita Hayworth poses in a black evening gown, elbow-length black gloves encasing her arms, drawing coolly on a cigarette. It was an image from the famous sequence 'Put the Blame On Mame', a seductive striptease which entices Glenn Ford and almost every other male in the audience into raptures for her. But artists' impressions of that image turn her into a wisp of smoke, a mirage from some magical lamp rather than a real woman. It was perhaps fair licence. For Hayworth was not so much the missing link between Harlow and Monroe, as is often claimed, but rather a unique personification of fantasies which crystallized around her figure in the mid-forties. She was a heightened version of a *femme fatale*, worthy of infinite sacrifice and casual betrayal. She was a reincarnation of World War One's Theda Bara, restyled for World War Two GIs into an image of unparalleled beauty which seemed in the end to destroy her. 'Every man I knew', she once said, 'had fallen in love with Gilda and wakened with me.'

She was born Margarita Cansino, daughter of a Spanish dancer, and related by marriage to Ginger Rogers. A teenage dancer and bit-part movie actress, she did not really emerge from the shadows until she was twenty-one when her first husband got her a contract at Columbia. Reincarnated as Hayworth, now a dyed redhead with a hairline raised by electrolysis, she got her first break with Howard Hawks' *Only Angels Have Wings*, 1939. Then she settled into a niche as the 'other woman' in *Strawberry Blonde, Affectionately Yours*, and most triumphantly opposite Tyrone Power in *Blood and Sand*, all 1941. She also kept up her talent as a highly effective dancer, partnering Fred Astaire in *You'll Never Get Rich*, 1941, and *You Were Never Lovelier*, 1942, and co-starring with Victor Mature in *My Gal Sal*, 1942, and Gene Kelly in *Cover Girl*, 1944.

RIGHT: publicity portrait for *Gilda*, 1946.
Photographer Robert W. Coburn

But *Gilda* was the image that stayed with her. Opposite Glenn Ford her agile face, full lips and flowing locks glowed like luminous jewels; he was subtly chosen to contrast, a bullish, squat, almost ugly partner, as earthbound as any man in the audience might feel when confronted with her charms. Orson Welles, the second of five husbands, came closest to re-creating that effect in his dazzling *The Lady from Shanghai*, 1948, filmed as they were filing for divorce. Hayworth in the title role is mysterious and predatory, deviously cruel; her hair

RIGHT: publicity portrait for *You'll Never Get Rich*, 1941, with Fred Astaire.
Photographer A. L. 'Whitey' Schaefer
BELOW: publicity portrait for *The Lady from Shanghai*, 1948, with Orson Welles.
Photographer Robert W. Coburn

was chopped off and dyed blonde for the part. It is a bitter, hateful, but erotically powerful movie. In a posed still from the famous shoot-out in the hall of mirrors, Welles grasps her close to him. She tilts her head back and seems to mock him, as if he is only holding her reflection in his arms.

It was perhaps her key role. It was in any case the last that she was able to play with genuine passion. A well-publicized but stormy two-year marriage to Prince Aly Khan in 1949 lasted long enough to wreck her association with Columbia and apparently to kill off the spark which brought her alive on screen. She was soon pleading with

LEFT: *The Loves of Carmen*, 1948, with Glenn Ford
BELOW: *Affair in Trinidad*, 1952, with Glenn Ford

Harry Cohn to allow her to return to her old studio, and she went on to earn herself a lot of money but little satisfaction. As if playing safe, the studio cast her in roles as *Salome*, 1953, and *Miss Sadie Thompson*, 1953, and these settled her into a run-of-the-mill Hollywood slot that contrasted sadly with her position for almost a decade on some sort of Olympian plinth. Many movies followed, but only *Pal Joey*, 1957, with Frank Sinatra could really claim to be anything approaching special.

Hayworth started out as the very epitome of glamour, a perfect incarnation of a Hollywood 'love goddess' who ruled the world. During the war, her 'Life' magazine pictures were printed in millions and despatched to troops on the front line. To them, she was a symbol – and this was more true of her than of many who have acquired that label – of a far-off world of sex, satin sheets, nightclubs, cigarette smoke, booze, and fast, dangerous women on the dance floor. But as the post-war world stabilized into one of

family duties and television, her purpose and essence seemed to evaporate, much like the wisp of smoke that had symbolized her most famous role. As the years went by, her private life became a protracted story of self-destruction and personal tragedy.

OPPOSITE: studio portrait, 1941.
Photographer A. L. 'Whitey' Schaefer
ABOVE: publicity portrait for *Salome*, 1953, with Stewart Granger.
Photographer Robert W. Coburn

145

DEBORAH KERR

LEFT: *Hatter's Castle*, 1941

The perfect role for Deborah Kerr came when she was just twenty-one, in the Michael Powell–Emeric Pressburger production *The Life and Death of Colonel Blimp*, 1942. She plays not one but three roles, as the eternally recurring love of Roger Livesey. She was prim and polite, as all English girls were supposed to be, but her red hair performed some chemical magic with the Technicolor process and she appeared – as she was supposed to appear – like an obsessive vision of loveliness. Audiences could not get her out of their minds either, and she was soon on her way to Hollywood. Before leaving she made *I See a Dark Stranger*, 1946, and played a memorable nun in *Black Narcissus*, 1947.

Kerr tended to veer between suppressed roles like nuns, schoolma'ams, widows or spinsters, and looser, more passionate women. After stepping into the classy shoes of Greer Garson at MGM, she broke away from type by taking on the role of the lusty wife in *From Here to Eternity*, 1953, for which she won the second of six Oscar nominations. Despite the acclaim, she somehow seemed more convincing as the English governess in *The King and I*, 1956, opposite Yul Brynner, or perhaps as the shipwrecked nun stranded on a desert island with Robert Mitchum in *Heaven Knows, Mr Allison*, 1957. There she managed to unite both the severe and the liberated sides of her character, and she built on her achievement in *Separate Tables*, 1958, with David Niven, and *The Sundowners*, 1960, again with Mitchum. Her keynote was an English reserve and restraint; so it was doubly exciting to hear her heartbeat quicken as Mitchum made his romantic advances.

OPPOSITE: publicity portrait for *The Killers*, 1946.
Photographer Ray Jones

Ava Gardner was a 'Hemingway woman': strong-willed, impetuous, magnetically sensual, a beauty who seemed at home among admiring men, but who never seemed to give in too easily to anyone. She was a throwback to Hemingway's world of tough-guy mystique, which seemed to bore her as much as it did her more youthful audiences. In a famous interview with columnist Rex Reed in the sixties, she looked back over her career and was blunt in assessing her achievements: 'Hell, baby, after twenty-five years in this business, if all you've got to show for it is *Mogambo* and *The Hucksters* you might as well give up.' On that evidence she was probably her own best scriptwriter, and her glamorous public persona as a late 1940s rival to Hayworth – 'The World's Most Exciting Animal' as one publicist would have it – was a reluctant achievement, a sop to the powers-that-be. She had grown from a nineteen-year-old MGM contract player at $50 per week back in 1941 to a wealthy jet-setting woman of the world, and she played that role to the hilt. In between she made short-lived marriages to Mickey Rooney, bandleader Artie Shaw, and Frank Sinatra. With its front-page quarrels, that last romance probably had more Hollywood-style drama and tragedy in it than most of her movies. And at times, she seemed to know as much.

Until 1946 she had been used to years of bit-parts and fifth-billing, and then she donned black satin dress and gloves for publicity for her new movie, *The Killers*. She exuded just the right aura of sultry elegance as a *femme fatale* opposite another promising newcomer, Burt Lancaster, and she contrived an attractive but laconic laziness that might have been caught from Robert Mitchum. It was an intelligent version of a Hemingway story,

ABOVE: publicity portrait for *The Killers*, 1946, with Burt Lancaster.
Photographer Ray Jones
RIGHT: *Mogambo*, 1953, with Clark Gable
OPPOSITE: publicity portrait for *My Forbidden Past*, 1951, with Robert Mitchum.
Photographer Ernest A. Bachrach

and it established her as a star; movies like *The Hucksters*, 1947, opposite Gable and Deborah Kerr followed. But it was not until she starred in *My Forbidden Past*, 1951, as a Southern belle opposite Mitchum himself, that her particular talent for the don't-give-a-damn look was again required.

She was most often cast as some paradoxical monument to her own beauty. She was required to be suitably mythical in the surrealistic *Pandora and the Flying Dutchman*, 1951, and played the half-caste lead in *Show Boat*, 1951 in which, to her fury, her own singing voice was dubbed. She played a 'Hemingway woman' opposite Gregory Peck in *The Snows of Kilimanjaro*, 1952, in which both managed to act like mobile versions of Mount Rushmore. *Mogambo*, 1953, gave her a crack at Jean Harlow's old role in *Red Dust* and an Oscar nomination, as she entices Clark Gable away from a safe option. But it was Joseph Mankiewicz's *The Barefoot Contessa*, 1954, with Humphrey Bogart, that best summed up her personality as a fiery Spanish dancer who becomes a Hollywood legend. This, and her part in *Bhowani Junction*, 1956, as a half-caste Indian, were her best roles. Her salary continued to increase but her interest seemed to lapse, though she gave some credible performances in fairly mediocre movies during the late fifties, sixties and seventies; in *The Night of the Iguana*, 1964, she had exactly the sort of earthy, sleazy role she always liked best.

LEFT: studio portrait. c. 1952.
Photographer Virgil Apger

Anna Magnani has an arresting face on which is written much of her history. The illegitimate child of an Egyptian and an Italian, and born in Alexandria, she took to the Italian stage in music-hall comedies, specializing in singing bawdy songs. Her intense look, staring eyes and shock of hair allowed for extremes of emotion, and she was a popular figure among American troops after the liberation of Rome. She had played minor roles since her first appearance on the screen in 1927, but she burst on the international scene in Roberto Rossellini's *Roma Città aperta*, 1945, giving a searing portrayal of a widow who is shot by the Germans. The tragedy seemed to sum up the passions of a whole generation of Italians after the war. Though the film was first decried in Italy, Magnani became internationally renowned and quickly went from strength to strength. She became a favourite actress of Rossellini (*L'Amore*, 1948), of Luchino Visconti, who directed her in the comic satire *Bellissima*, 1951, and of Jean Renoir, who chose her for *La Carrozza d'Oro*, 1953. She went to Hollywood to make a film especially written for her by Tennessee Williams, *The Rose Tattoo*, 1955, and won an Oscar as Best Actress. Further triumphs followed, in Europe and the USA: she played opposite Marlon Brando in *The Fugitive Kind*, 1960, and was the centrepiece of Pasolini's *Mamma Roma*, 1962. But by the end of the fifties her career was in decline. Her face, racked by experience and suffering, and her emotionalized acting style were both out of vogue, and audiences opted for the less troublesome ways of the pneumatic Lollobrigida and Loren; their slum-girl appeal could be tastefully transmuted into a covetable image of bikinis, pop music and Vespas, an image to which Magnani was safely immune.

ABOVE: *Il Bandito*, 1946, with Amedeo Nazzari

Judy Garland always retained the magic that rubbed off from *The Wizard of Oz*, 1939. Beautiful, fresh and appealing as Mickey Rooney's sweetheart in *Strike Up the Band*, 1940, it was somehow appalling that, by the time of *A Star is Born*, 1954, she should be so visibly racked by the real traumas and cracked lines of adulthood. Her persona was always balanced precariously between those two extremes. The tragic story of her reliance on drugs and the collapse of her career is well known; and yet she achieved some of the purest screen definitions of romance.

Meet Me in St Louis, 1944, is, of course, a sweet-toothed reminder of her days as a juvenile hoofer *à la* Shirley Temple. But *The Pirate*, 1947, with Gene Kelly is a dashingly exuberant parody of swashbuckling folk, in which Garland's Technicolor dreams of love with her phantom pirate make one almost giddy with colour, movement and sheer energy. But it was a little-remembered movie, *The Clock*, 1945, also directed by her second husband Vincente Minnelli, in which she gave one of her strongest performances. Unlike many of the movies for which Garland is famous, it is a real-life fairy-tale filmed in black and white, without the benefit of songs. It is Garland who provides the film's soaring heights and intensity. She plays a young girl who falls in love with soldier Robert Walker on twenty-four-hour leave in New York. The panic in her eyes when she thinks she has lost him is unforgettable: it brings memories of how in her best music her heart seems to swell until it might burst, and is reminiscent of the sense of fear and elation that pervades a vintage silent like *Sunrise*. Garland may have made better movies, but she never had a stronger sense of hope.

OPPOSITE: publicity portrait for *The Clock*, 1945, with Robert Walker
ABOVE: *Words and Music*, 1948, with Mickey Rooney
LEFT: studio portrait, 1957. Photographer John Engstead

JANE RUSSELL

From the moment in 1946 that a San Francisco skywriting plane drew two circles in the sky with dots in the middle, Jane Russell must have known that she would be haunted by the publicity campaign for *The Outlaw* for the rest of her life. The ample breasts of this young chiropodist's assistant from Minnesota were the two reasons why the red-blooded males of America were roused to 'tussle with Russell', and why the Legion of Decency delayed the film's official release for nine years. Russell's sex-bomb persona produced hysteria but it was to obscure her real talents as a comedienne.

Her most famous role as Dorothy in

Gentlemen Prefer Blondes, 1953, teamed her with Marilyn Monroe, both resplendent in top hats, tassels and fishnets and bashing out the sophisticated sexual ironies of Anita Loos' story. Russell's bamboozling qualities had emerged most hilariously opposite a flustered Bob Hope in *Paleface*, 1948, and *Son of Paleface*, 1952. Unfortunately the rest of her career was short on both irony and sophistication, typecast as she was as the too-hot-to-handle woman that GIs craved. Her leading men were picked from the 'I've-been-to-hell-and-back' category: Robert Mitchum in *His Kind of Woman*, 1951, and *Macao*, 1953, and both Vincent Price and Victor Mature in

the lurid *The Las Vegas Story*, 1952. At her most crudely mythical she played the title role in *The Revolt of Mamie Stover*, 1956, a nostalgic film about the famous Second World War Honolulu 'madame' who organized sexual 'rest 'n' recreation' for a generation of war-weary GIs. Howard Hughes had lured her from obscurity for *The Outlaw* and was still renewing her $1,000-per-week contract in the early 1970s. Perhaps she thought of him when, after his death, she put her talents to advertising bras on television.

ABOVE: publicity portrait for *Young Widow*, 1945. Photographer George Hurrell

Cyd Charisse had the most eloquent legs in show business. While other actresses struggled with the Method or wrestled with hack dialogue, Charisse's legs possessed a range of vocabulary and expression that went beyond Funk & Wagnell's Dictionary. When teamed with Fred Astaire in *The Band Wagon*, 1953, she rivalled and even surpassed his fluidity and elegance, producing a combination of confidence and ability that could have outshone even that of Ginger Rogers. And while Gene Kelly made up for lack of inspiration by sheer hard work in *Singin' in the Rain*, 1952, and *It's Always Fair Weather*, 1955, Charisse stole scenes with ease, goading Kelly's musclebound legs with one cool kick of her silk-clad limbs.

Charisse was Texas born and ballet trained, and she signed with MGM in 1946. In the movies, though, sheer talent isn't always enough. Charisse was perfect for Cinemascope, for her legs could extend the full width of the frame, but her favoured partner Astaire was better suited to the squarer, Academy format in black and white, while Kelly was dwarfed by her; so Charisse lacked a suitable leading man with whom to develop a screen persona. In Vincente Minnelli's *Brigadoon*, 1954, with Kelly and in *Silk Stockings*, 1957, with Astaire, in which she played Garbo's old Ninotchka

role, the pace had slowed down to a lumbering gait. It was left to director Nicholas Ray to provide her with a peach of a part in *Party Girl*, 1958, a pepped-up version of a gangster movie which hinted at a talent for heavier duty dramatic roles. She returned to Minnelli for a part as Kirk Douglas' ex-wife in *Two Weeks in Another Town*, 1962, but although she was good, she was under-used; and since the full-scale MGM musical showed no signs of making a comeback, Charisse left Hollywood for Europe and the night-club stage.

ABOVE: *The Band Wagon*, 1953, with Fred Astaire

KAY KENDALL

Kay Kendall was one of those model Knightsbridge-style girls in jewels and furs who showed an unexpected zest for sophisticated comedy. At her best some murmured a comparison with Carole Lombard, but even if she didn't quite hit those heights, Kendall made a lasting impression as a vivacious and skilful comedienne in her few major film roles before her death from leukaemia in 1959, when she was still only thirty-three.

She was in fact not born in London's elegant West End, but in the Yorkshire port of Hull; her parents were both dancers. Aged twelve she joined the chorus at the London Palladium and made it into bit-parts in films, then rose to fame quite unexpectedly in *Genevieve*, 1953, as a classy model forced into crazy situations by Kenneth More during a vintage car race. It was a quaint film of whimsical appeal, but she was a smash hit, particularly when she demonstrated her own natural talent as a trumpeter in a jazz club scene. She continued to show her potential opposite Dirk Bogarde in *Doctor in the House*, 1954, Peter Finch in *Simon and Laura*, and Rex Harrison in *The Constant Husband*, both 1955. Kendall and Harrison formed a perfect match both on screen and off, and she became the third Mrs Harrison in 1957. One can imagine a whole series of debonair comedies, slightly genteel, slightly old-fashioned, starring them both; but their only joint effort was Minnelli's *The Reluctant Debutante*, 1958, which unfortunately did not set the world alight. Her most promising role was with Gene Kelly in Cukor's *Les Girls*, 1957, in which Kendall showed her flair for musical comedy with a sure touch. It prompted great expectations for the future, so her death was widely grieved.

LEFT: studio portrait, 1954.
Photographer Cornell Lucas

DORIS DAY

JANE WYMAN

Doris Day was one of those fixtures of the American home in the early fifties. Outside was the cruel world of the Korean War and the atomic bomb; but inside was an advertisement from 'Good Housekeeping', with Doris in the kitchen – blonde, bobbed, and as pert as a kitten. In *Calamity Jane*, 1953, and *The Pajama Game*, 1957, she had been capable of a wild energy as a singer and dancer that gave her a Ginger Rogers-style brittleness, and status as one of the first teenage idols; but when she sided with decency and independence against bamboozling males – like Rock Hudson in *Pillow Talk*, 1959, then later Cary Grant and James Garner – she developed an image which stuck throughout the swinging sixties as the girl who would always say 'No'.

BELOW: *Julie*, 1956, with Louis Jourdan

One can barely think of Jane Wyman without a glycerine tear sliding down the cheek, for she established an un-equalled reputation as a sob-sister from the moment she won an Oscar in *Johnny Belinda*, 1948, for her part as a seventeen-year-old deaf mute. The fact that she was all of thirty-four, and about to divorce husband Ronald Reagan, did not detract from the sheer winsomeness of it all. In Sirk's *Magnificent Obsession*, 1954, she took on the old Irene Dunne role as a woman blinded by a reckless playboy (Rock Hudson); and then fell in love with Hudson again in *All That Heaven Allows*, 1955. Both movies painted the nightmare side of suburban life in strong colours, and Wyman's presence had the bitter taste of saccharin.

ABOVE: *All That Heaven Allows*, 1955, with Rock Hudson

GLORIA GRAHAME

Gloria Grahame played a whole series of parts which summed up much of that early fifties mood of weary cynicism. She was a new kind of woman: unattached, floating, perhaps with some unlucky story lurking in her background. It always seemed as if she had been out at some party, and was now slightly raw and hungover but determined to find her kicks where and when she could. That marvellous cracked voice of her was used to full advantage opposite Bogart in *In a Lonely Place*, 1950. She was a revelation, not quite twenty-five years old, a next-door neighbour who helps Bogart clear his name of murder. She displayed a sour wit, delivered straight on,

and deserved more parts like it. Its director Nicholas Ray was the second of her four husbands, and she had previously starred for him in *A Woman's Secret*, 1949; but even he didn't always seem able to match her talent to the right material.

Her first big success after signing with MGM was as a singer in *Crossfire*, 1947, for which she was Oscar nominated, and she quickly graduated to leading roles; but then got stuck. She appeared in DeMille's *The Greatest Show on Earth*, 1952, but returned to more favourable sweet-and-sour territory as a restless young wife to Dick Powell in Minnelli's *The Bad and the Beautiful*, 1952, for which she won

an Oscar as Best Supporting Actress. She was sensational in *The Big Heat*, 1953, when she beat a retreat to homely Glenn Ford after having coffee flung in her face by the psychopathic Lee Marvin; and she was given a major role in Minnelli's *The Cobweb*, 1955, only to see her rival stars ruin a delicately wrought scenario. She lacked that plastic 'all-mod-cons' look which was then all the rage: the world of late fifties gloss just wasn't sympathetic to her talents. Thus her career peaked but briefly, and until her death in 1982 she played minor roles on stage, screen and television.

ABOVE: *Human Desire*, 1954

There are two Janet Leighs. The confident blonde who starred in brash Technicolor epics and adventures of the fifties seems to bear little relation to the actress who is a central part of three classic thrillers made at the end of that decade: Orson Welles' *Touch of Evil*, 1958, Alfred Hitchcock's *Psycho*, 1960, and John Frankenheimer's *The Manchurian Candidate*, 1962, all three baroque fantasies in black and white.

She had been discovered by Norma Shearer, and was given an MGM contract on Shearer's personal recommendation. She emerged as a solid actress, somewhat bland, but with good parts in tough action pictures like *The Naked Spur*, 1953, or in costume dramas like *Scaramouche*, 1952, and *Prince Valiant*, 1954. Husband Tony Curtis was her co-star in two more extravaganzas, *The Black Shield of Falworth*, 1954, and that masterpiece of camp *The Vikings*, 1958, but they had been more profitably teamed in the earlier *Houdini*, 1953.

Throughout the fifties Leigh was a major star, and it was therefore all the more remarkable that she should accept the part of Charlton Heston's threatened wife in *Touch of Evil*, where she is terrorized by a gang in a motel room. There must have been something about Leigh and motels: in *Psycho* she even breathes her last in one, killed half-way through the film by Anthony Perkins in that famous shower sequence. These two films, and *The Manchurian Candidate*, played her against type, challenging the audience's expectations of her as a safe heroine bound to have a happy ending. She continued in movies during the sixties (she and Curtis divorced in 1962), but never matched this remarkable trio. She did, however, appear in *The Fog*, 1979 with her beautiful daughter, Jamie Lee Curtis.

ABOVE: *Psycho*, 1960, with John Gavin

GRACE KELLY

Grace Kelly was always regarded as a valuable jewel: ice-cold, hard and glacial, sparkling, serene and timeless. She was regarded as Hollywood aristocracy even before proving herself as an actress, and her ascent to the fairy-tale heights of Princess Grace of Monaco was entirely in accordance with her personality and public image. She was somewhat too cool as Gary Cooper's wife in *High Noon*, 1952, and limpid opposite Gable and Ava Gardner in *Mogambo*, 1953, but she was the precise focus for Alfred Hitchcock's desires in an important trio of movies.

He once referred to his taste, where women were concerned, for 'the drawing-room type, the real ladies, who become whores once they're in the bedroom'. And, a voyeuristic glee in her fate notwithstanding, that is how he presents her in *Dial M for Murder*, 1954, where she is almost strangled; in *Rear Window*, 1954, in which she offers an invalided James Stewart a provocative come-on in her nightgown; and in *To Catch a Thief*, 1955, where she is decidedly upper-crust opposite Cary Grant. She is quite likeable in all these, with a sex appeal best likened to that of ice thawing; but she appears virtually oblivious to the sadistic innuendo implicit in the way she was being observed by her director. Amongst the dross in which she appeared before her famous marriage in 1956, her role in *High Society*, 1956, stands out. Her dove-like rendition of 'True Love' with Bing Crosby compensated for any static elegance in the former Katharine Hepburn role. It was actually a better performance than that in *The Country Girl*, 1954, also with Crosby, for which she won a Best Actress Oscar.

ABOVE: publicity portrait for *Rear Window*, 1954.
    Photographer Bud Fraker
LEFT: publicity for *To Catch a Thief*, 1955, with
    Cary Grant
OPPOSITE: studio portrait, 1954.
    Photographer Bud Fraker

THE 'NEW LOOK'

In the aftermath of the Second World War, the major Hollywood studios found that the movie business would not remain their private fiefdom for much longer. They had lost their vital cinema theatre monopoly after a Supreme Court ruling in 1948. Then gradually they began to realize that the attention of America's leisured classes was falling away from the big screen. Their fellow patriot Senator McCarthy had named Communism as the Number One Enemy; but the Hollywood bosses knew that the *real* enemy was television.

TV – the little 'tube', the 'one-eyed monster', the 'chewing gum for the eyes' – was the medium whose name they hardly dared mention. The context was post-war America, where the home and family life in general were becoming the dominant focus. The newly-named 'nuclear family' shut the doors on the world and spent money on refrigerators, gramophones, furniture and automobiles – all the consumer goods being advertised on television. The logic was irrefutable. 'Why should people go out and pay money to see a bad film,' said Sam Goldwyn, 'when they can stay at home and see bad TV for nothing?'

The response of Hollywood to this new enemy was as simple as it was simple-minded. The movies had to make the most of their strengths and become larger than life. Big was suddenly Beautiful, and the quest for bigger screens, greater epics and larger audiences became something of an obsession. The 3-D *Bwana Devil*, 1952 ('A Lion in Your Lap' ran the slogan), was released in the same year as *This Is Cinerama* offered a three-screen roller-coaster ride; *The Robe*, 1953, announced the arrival of the more successful Cinema-Scope, while *Around the World in Eighty Days*, 1956, brought the spectacular process of 70mm Todd-AO to the world's attention.

In Europe, however, attention had been focussed on a different kind of 'New Look'. Christian Dior's 1947 collection of fashion designs had swept away the wartime utility clothing and austerity rations and put in its place a bold new emphasis on the female form. A tiny wasp waist, a tight slender bodice, curved shoulders, rounded bosoms and full hips made for a pneumatic silhouette of high style and glamour which seemed more-Hollywood-than-Hollywood. Its revolutionary stress on femininity, or at least on Dior's stylized version of it, proved magnetically popular even beyond the confines of the Parisian world of *haute couture*. It became a symbol of post-war liberation. In a few years Dior's 'New Look' had been adapted, plagiarized and vulgarized into the familiar stereotype of the big-busted wiggling blonde. Here too, Big was definitely Beautiful.

The fusion of this 'New Look' and the new nuclear age came in the phenomenon of the Sex-Bomb. Loren, Mangano and Lollobrigida stepped out of the war-torn back streets of Italy into the atomic age of bubblegum, television, nylons, pop music, drip-dry shirts and frozen food. Like their counterparts in America, they flaunted sex as yet another consumer item, were supposedly capable of explosive impact, and catered for an infantile male obsession with large breasts. America herself specialized in blondes, pumped up and pneumatic like a shiny new Cadillac, with high-pitched, breathy giggling to substitute for speech. Marilyn Monroe developed her own version from a Harlow mould, but added a nervous individuality which was lacking from her imitators. Jayne Mansfield parodied the role for laughs; Mamie van Doren was the B-movie version, Diana Dors the British; Anita Ekberg was the Miss Sweden and Miss Universe contender; Kim Novak was 'Miss Deep-Freeze'; and Carroll Baker played the ultimate child-wife as a *Baby Doll*, 1956, all short nightdresses and sucking her thumb.

Brigitte Bardot was different again. She had played bit-parts in many movies before becoming an international star in her then husband Roger Vadim's *Et Dieu créa la femme/And God Created Woman*, 1956. Her long blond hair went with a freer, more Bohemian spirit. Her lack of make-up marked the Hollywood badges of glossed lips and painted nails as signs of conformity. Her petulant sexuality seemed instinctively precocious, and she questioned social morality and ethics in a lazily seductive manner. With a St Tropez lifestyle of unthinking hedonism, she opened up a door to the 1960s – even though her heavily publicized image as a pouting sex kitten belonged rather to fifties infantilism.

Paradoxically perhaps, the vogue for boyish looks with slim figures and flat chests became popular at the same time that Big was Beautiful. Audrey Hepburn set a wholly new trend that allowed for the *gamine* style of Leslie Caron, the emaciated look of Jean Seberg, and the kookiness of the red-headed Shirley MacLaine. For cinema was a series of contradictions during the 1950s, fired by its quest for *more* of everything. It became more vulgar, more sensitive, more youthful, more safe, more colourful, more exuberant, yet more grown-up all at the same time.

The assault on convention was from all sides. Directors like Otto Preminger and Stanley Kramer pushed for the treatment of controversial, adult subjects in such films as *The Moon is Blue*, 1953 (in which the word 'virgin' brought complaints from the Legion of Decency), *The Man With the Golden Arm*, 1955, *On the Beach*, 1959, and *Judgment at Nuremberg*, 1961. The New York Actors' Studio, founded in 1948, trained a whole generation of actors and actresses in the Stanislavsky style of acting known as The Method: Marlon Brando, James Dean, Montgomery Clift, Paul Newman, Rod Steiger, Joanne Woodward and more all changed the range and mood of performances on screen. The older generation of actresses was confused by this taut, nervous energy, and the casual style of dress with T-shirt and blue jeans. 'I don't believe you want to go to the theatre', said Joan Crawford in a famous quotation, 'to see somebody you can see next door.' But younger audiences wanted just that. As rock 'n' roll and black rhythms invaded the starched white world of pop, the young consumers known as teenagers wanted to see their own adolescent and neurotic sub-culture reflected up there on the screen; for they knew the world was now divided into young and old. Dean in *Rebel Without a Cause*, 1955, and Brando, leather-jacketed, in *The Wild One*, 1953, talked about gangs, teenage problems and sex, and became icons that preached resentment of authority.

This confrontation between rock 'n' roll and the movies was heavily ironic. Only thirty years ago, cinema had been the sinful medium, expressing shamelessly the hopes and fears of young Americans; by the 1950s it had become identified with an old-fashioned, authoritarian, parental view, and had to discover from outsiders how to keep up to date. Even if Coca-Cola and Cadillacs with fins shout 'fifties America' to modern youth, cinema in the era of Eisenhower most properly belonged to the 'squares'. It was a world of Debbie Reynolds and Doris Day, of Grace Kelly, Bar-B-Qs and country clubs – a narrow, conservative, Republican world in which aliens of any kind rarely appeared, except in the avidly scaremongering science-fiction movies which alerted all true Americans to beware of invaders from hostile planets.

Signs of stress in the industry were evident in the rejuvenation of established genres, of the Western with *The Searchers*, 1956, and *3.10 to Yuma*, 1957, or of the Melodrama, like *Written On the Wind*, 1956, and *Imitation of Life*, 1958. For perhaps in these supposedly safe formats, directors and writers felt less compelled to aim for novelty and more able to suggest complexities, ambiguities and doubts about their world. There was at the same time a sense of strain and disorder within the industry itself, as producers increasingly worked independently of the studios, making single pictures instead of whole cycles under one studio roof. There was a growing freedom, but also more deliberation about what to make.

As Hollywood moved into the mid-sixties, it was difficult not to feel that the party was very nearly over. For the public, cinema was now one medium of entertainment among many. It had to compete with television, pop music, bowling alleys, sporting events, or just driving around in the latest model of car, for consumers' money. And when forced to compete, it generally lagged behind other industries, proving itself unable to satisfy whims fast enough or to anticipate trends. The old Hollywood more or less remained as a shadow of its former glory. Clark Gable, James Stewart, Cary Grant all made movies into their fifties and sixties, but their appeal proved inimitable by the actors intended to replace them. Female stars enjoyed nothing like this longevity, although Elizabeth Taylor did remain as a pinnacle of the *ancien régime*. Despite isolated glories and rushes of enthusiasm, the movie business was left facing modern times in poor shape.

SOPHIA LOREN

By the time Sophia Loren was in her mid-twenties, she'd seen it all. Like a character from a Fellini movie or Visconti's *Bellissima*, she escaped from the post-war poverty of Italy into a life of vapid glamour by courtesy of those hardy perennial fairy-tale characters, the pushy mother, the father-figure producer. She started out as a streetwise waif, developed into an attractive accessory to ageing American stars, and hit the headlines as a fully-fledged Hollywood-style 'sex-bomb'. It was no surprise that by the mid-sixties she should have taken on another role as the sophisticated woman of the world: her capacity for survival, if nothing else, had earned her it.

Born illegitimately into the war-ravaged slums of Naples as Sofia Scicolone, by the age of fourteen she was hustling at the film studios in Rome for work. She was very beautiful and very hungry, an urchin with eyes grown large through gazing at food through shop windows. By the time she was sixteen, fate had intervened in the form of film producer Carlo Ponti. He took her up and made her a star in the Hollywood mould, launching her in Italy as if she were some unexpected benefit of Marshall Aid.

By 1954 Loren was established as a serious rival to Lollobrigida, for the Loren–Ponti portrayal of poverty was usually a case of parading Sophia before the cameras in a wet blouse. Loren and Ponti married in 1957, but the courts' refusal to recognize Ponti's divorce began a nine-year legal battle.

Meanwhile, Loren pouted and preened through Stanley Kramer's *The Pride and the Passion*, 1957, and went to Hollywood in the following year. There, *It Started in Naples*, 1960, teamed her with an ageing Clark Gable. Only with *El Cid*, 1961, and *Heller in Pink Tights*, 1960, did Loren find directors like Anthony Mann and George Cukor who could get her best from her. And opposite Jean-Paul Belmondo in De Sica's *La Ciociara/Two Women*, 1960, she proved her ambitions as an actress by winning an Oscar for her performance as a woman on the run

ABOVE: publicity for *The Pride and the Passion*, 1957.
Photographer Ken Danvers
OPPOSITE: studio portrait, 1956.
Photographer Ken Danvers

with her child in wartime Italy. That acclaim at last allowed her to transcend her busty, fifties image.

After 1960 she worked only in Europe, escaping adoption as a glamour queen by opting for sophisticated sex comedies like *Matrimonio all' Italiana*, 1964, with Marcello Mastroianni. In her earliest films she possessed a bold Italian charm, but by the time she had been repackaged, sweetened and exported, she had turned bland. Like canned spaghetti, she remained popular despite being but a memory of her former self.

RIGHT: *Legend of the Lost*, 1957, with
John Wayne
BELOW: *Matrimonio all'Italiana*, 1964, with
Marcello Mastroianni

If Anna Magnani showed how neo-realist films could be both moving and socially conscious, then Silvana Mangano was the actress who showed how a social conscience could be mingled with intense eroticism, even in the most painful stories of post-war misery. As a fresh-faced nineteen-year-old she became internationally famous in *Riso Amaro/Bitter Rice*, 1949, in which the audience's awareness of the agonies of peasant life came a poor second to its awareness of Mangano herself, as she toiled in the rice fields up to her thighs in water. She was sultry, passionate, and a huge hit; and after marrying the film's producer Dino De Laurentiis, she established herself as Italy's leading young actress.

That position did not last long. With the rise of Loren and Lollobrigida, Mangano slipped into third place; but while they drifted into the international no-man's-land of sex comedies, rugged action yarns and routine thrillers, Mangano took the opposite route. In *Edipo Re/Oedipus Rex*, 1967, as Jocasta and in *Teorema*, 1968, she developed a persona under the direction of Pier Paolo Pasolini that was strange and unearthly, hauntingly tragic. By her mid-thirties she was proving capable of a depth and maturity in performance which audiences found remarkable, and she continued to grow in stature. In Visconti's *Morte a Venezia/Death in Venice*, 1971, her whitened face resembled a death-mask recently brought back to life, and she continued her collaborations with that director in *Ludwig*, 1972, and *Gruppo di Famiglia in un Interno/Conversation Piece*, 1974. In this she excels as a slightly decadent aristocrat, with a careful hauteur contradicting her outwardly languid smile.

ABOVE: *Riso Amaro*, 1949
RIGHT: *Morte a Venezia*, 1971

GINA LOLLOBRIGIDA

Along with the Vespa, espresso coffee, and her deadly enemy Sophia Loren, Gina Lollobrigida was one of Italy's most popular exports in the fifties. An ex-model, she exemplified a style of naïve confidence and calculated ambition which brought her quickly to international attention. Her nickname 'La Lollo' became a by-word for a kind of sluttish glamour that was a strange compromise between a good Italian girl's unselfconscious beauty and the vision of loveliness dreamt up by platoons of sex-starved GIs. In her early roles she managed somehow to suggest both in films like *Pane, Amore e Fantasia/Bread, Love and Dreams*, 1953, and in René Clair's *Les Belles de nuit*, 1952, and *La Romana*, 1954. Her casting as Bogart's sexy wife in the quirky *Beat the Devil*, 1954, opened Hollywood's eyes to her charms, but a continuing dispute over an earlier contract with Howard Hughes forced her to work in Europe. She was Esmeralda to a hunchbacked Anthony Quinn in *Notre Dame de Paris*, 1956, and was suitably upholstered as the Queen of Sheba opposite Yul Brynner in the gaudy Biblical epic *Solomon and Sheba*, 1959.

But any acting ambitions were quickly sacrificed to the era's bizarre breast fixation. From the early days, her ample bosom was given a starring role as a promise of pneumatic bliss, and her persona became dedicated to this singular obsession. Movies like *Anna di Brooklyn/Fast and Sexy*, 1958, and *Go Naked in the World*, 1960, became increasingly irrelevant compared to her off-screen antics to create publicity headlines, as if she were merely a walking advertisement for her own charms. In recent years, she has taken a spirited revenge by taking up a position behind the camera as a professional photographer.

LEFT: publicity portrait for *Go Naked in the World*, 1960.
Photographer Virgil Apger

OPPOSITE: studio portrait, 1953.
Photographer Gene Kornman

Now that her image is available on everything from pillowcases and hamburgers to posters and fine art, Marilyn Monroe may be said to have transcended her own time once and for all. She has entered the dizzy realm of twentieth-century myth as an American icon, a leading lady to the world, whose likeness has been novelized by Norman Mailer, painted by Andy Warhol, and impersonated by thousands of drag acts all over the world. Yet although her pouting lips, wiggling walk and platinum blonde hair are familiar to most who have not lived inside a vault for the last thirty years, in this context it is worth recalling just how *ordinary* her rise to fame was.

It was, after all, a traditional starlet's rise, after a famously unhappy childhood. Illegitimate, with a mentally ill mother, Norma Jean Mortenson lived in a series of foster homes and orphanages until she escaped, aged sixteen, by marriage. Her rise to fame began with model work, her brown hair now bleached and bobbed, and she made a slow start as an actress, suffering bit-parts, walk-ons and unrenewed contracts in five years of good and bad. She was pursued by Groucho Marx in *Love Happy*, 1949, patronized by George Sanders in *All About Eve*, 1950, and pacified by Richard Widmark in *Don't Bother to Knock*, 1952. Like a soft-centred, musical version of Harlow, she swept through leading roles in *Gentlemen Prefer Blondes* and *How to Marry a Millionaire*, both 1953, but still with elements of uncertainty visible amid the glamour and glitz of those productions. It was not until *The Seven Year Itch*, 1955, that she began to show the confidence expected of the major star she had become. Yet, oddly for such a supposedly all-American sex symbol, her personification of fifties eroticism came over as that of a dream girl from another planet: breathy, cartoon-like, streamlined, pneumatic. She sensed the desire for unreality, and made it flesh.

Her ambition to be considered as an actress rather than a glamour queen was understandable and not untypical of that era's vogue for seriousness; but she did show real acting talent in *Bus Stop*, 1956, in which her brittle sexiness was taken over by a genuine tenderness and affection. The trouble was that whenever she was poured

ABOVE: publicity portrait for *The Seven Year Itch*, 1955.
Photographer Frank Powolny
OPPOSITE: studio portrait, c. 1952

into a satin dress and primed to wiggle and giggle, the old Monroe myth returned without any bidding; *Some Like it Hot*, 1959, became a superb farce as a result. Only *The Misfits*, 1961, among her last films shows a maturing actress destined for greatness, and she is immensely moving next to another Hollywood icon, in the shape of Clark Gable, who seems about to expire with every breath.

By this time Monroe's personal problems were interfering with her professional life. Frequently ill, under psychiatric care and subject to extreme nerves before the cameras, Monroe could be hostile and aggressive. Her colleagues' impatience got her dismissed from the set of her last film, *Something's Got to Give*.

Her sad death a month later incarnated her as an exhibit in the pop museum of Americana, along with Elvis and Coca-Cola. She had associated with the brawn (Joe DiMaggio), the brain (Arthur Miller) and even with the uncrowned royalty of America, the Kennedys, and her yearning after the great symbols of American life and hope through the medium of movies seems in retrospect almost conscious. When one begins to realize that, and then takes stock of her undoubted talents and wasted life, it perhaps seems that there was little ordinary about Marilyn Monroe after all.

ABOVE: publicity portrait for *How to Marry a Millionaire*, 1953
RIGHT: publicity portrait for *The Prince and the Showgirl*, 1957.
Photographer Richard Avedon

As a young model Kim Novak played the part of 'Miss Deepfreeze', demonstrating refrigerators to eager purchasers. Was this just coincidence? The title is unerringly apt for this sad-eyed blonde with the icy smile, whom chance led to one of the greatest connoisseurs of the species, Alfred Hitchcock. Novak is the very core of his *Vertigo*, 1958, a swirling vortex of memory and obsession in which Novak's blandly anonymous features and hesitant air take on a mesmerizing force. The battle against her frozen inexpressiveness brings out a hitherto hidden warmth which engulfs her co-star James Stewart. Stewart's naturally gawky charm was the direct opposite of Novak's own appeal, and they teamed together again well in *Bell, Book and Candle*, also 1958.

This was her peak, when she displaced even Marilyn Monroe in the hearts of the American public; and it is tempting to say that her very blankness gave her the edge in popularity, for a short time at least. She had started out as Columbia's replacement for Rita Hayworth, and to many people's surprise the studio publicity campaign worked. She caught Sinatra's eye in *The Man With the Golden Arm*, and hit the big time opposite William Holden in *Picnic*, both 1955. Her screen charisma was low in *Pal Joey*, but she made up for it with the gutsy starring role as *Jeanne Eagels*, both 1957, a tinseltown booze-and-drugs biopic. She went through the motions of stardom and emerged on the giddy heights of *The Legend of Lylah Clare*, 1968, but in truth came over best opposite Dean Martin in Billy Wilder's satirical *Kiss Me, Stupid*, 1964, when even she seemed to be able to relax and take her star status more lightly.

RIGHT: *Jeanne Eagels*, 1957

SIMONE SIGNORET

In *Casque d'or*, 1952, Simone Signoret looks as though she has descended from a Renoir painting, all lace and elaborate jewellery, sparkling eyes and a flashing smile. Yet by the time she made *Room at the Top*, only seven years later, she is already the 'older woman', her face resonant with experience, proudly passionate and serious about love. Signoret belonged to a generation of French actresses for whom age did not mean losing looks but gaining experience; and it was for the latter that she was valued. She won a Best Actress Oscar for her role as the discarded lover of Laurence Harvey, and rightly so. For even as a fresh, young girl in her twenties, she had managed to communicate a sense of pain and worldly knowledge at which most actresses – and actors – could only guess.

After bit-parts in Paris during the Second World War, she rose to prominence in Max Ophüls' splendid *La Ronde*, 1950, quickly followed by *Casque d'or* and a role as the adulteress in Marcel Carné's *Thérèse Raquin*, 1953. She always seemed to play a woman from whom pleasure was sought illicitly, but managed to select her parts as prostitutes and good-time girls with discrimination. As one of the plotters in *Les Diaboliques*, 1955, she was effortlessly convincing; but in later years, notably in *Ship of Fools*, 1965, her woman-of-the-world role became clichéd and overblown. She was always suited to an era of strong commitments and seemed out of step with modern complacency. Her famous marriage to Yves Montand (her first was to director Yves Allégret) brought with it a real-life role as the female half of France's most glamorous left-wing couple.

ABOVE: *Thérèse Raquin*, 1953, with Raf Vallone
OPPOSITE: *Casque d'or*, 1952, with
Claude Dauphin

JEAN SIMMONS

As an early graduate of the Rank charm school, and a successful child star, Jean Simmons learned all those tricks of coy flirtatiousness that passed for a British version of post-war glamour. Luckily she possessed more ability than most. After earning acclaim as Estelle in *Great Expectations*, 1946, and an Oscar nomination as a blonde Ophelia opposite Olivier in *Hamlet*, 1948, she started to outgrow the naughty-but-nice-girl roles offered to her in Britain and moved to America, as the wife of Stewart Granger. There her poise and cool reserve became much in demand. She gives Robert Mitchum a characteristically limpid look in *Angel Face*, 1952, the film that showed for the first time her ability to switch from angel to devil within the space of a reel change; and after dutifully donning togas in some costume epics, she won an excellent part in the musical *Guys and Dolls*, 1955. As Sergeant Sarah, the girl from the Save-a-Soul Mission, she is hoodwinked by the roguish Sky Masterson (Marlon Brando) into flying to Havana. She is pert, strait-laced and stiff-upper-lipped opposite Brando's sly, streetwise 'Noo Yawker'; but the charm of the hilarious sequence lies in the way Simmons melts into a fun-loving girl with more than a twinkle in her eye, and in time to dance. That was played for laughs, but she was just as strong in more serious roles, and shone as the wayward evangelist in *Elmer Gantry*, 1960, directed by her second husband, Richard Brooks. Since *The Happy Ending*, 1969, which brought another Oscar nomination, Simmons has made only occasional appearances on screen or stage.

OPPOSITE: publicity portrait for *Hamlet*, 1948.
Photographer Wilfrid Newton
ABOVE: publicity portrait for *Adam and Evelyne*, 1949, with Stewart Granger
LEFT: *Until They Sail*, 1957, with Paul Newman

ELIZABETH TAYLOR

Unlike, say, Marilyn Monroe, whose whole existence seemed to resonate with the era of Eisenhower and of Kennedy's America, Elizabeth Taylor has never seemed representative of any special historical period or style. Instead she may be likened to a Hollywood star that has grown to incredible brightness but has found no sure direction, one that sucks bits of debris from other galaxies into its orbit. She is one of the last examples of that type of stardom. Her career has been erratic, wasteful and uncertain in all but ambition, and it is her private life – in particular her seven well-publicized marriages – that ousts her films as the main object of interest.

If she seems to have been with cinema audiences for a very long time, it is because of her childhood stardom that lasted from *Lassie Come Home*, 1943, and *National Velvet*, 1944, right up to her coming of age at eighteen as Spencer Tracy's daughter in *Father of the Bride*, 1950. Most of her best work falls within the next decade, and she changed films at only a slightly greater pace than her husbands: from Conrad Hilton Jr to Michael Wilding, from Mike Todd to Eddie Fisher, then from Richard Burton to Richard Burton and eventually to John Warner. Her romantic first in movies was Robert Taylor in *Conspirator*, 1949, but she proved better in roles that demanded more spirited histrionics. She was outstandingly desirable in *A Place in the Sun*, 1951, made a strong presence opposite James Dean in *Giant*, 1956, and was Oscar nominated for her performance opposite Montgomery Clift in *Raintree County*, 1957. She seemed to blossom in the face of Clift's neuroticism, for her own talent was for steamier, more bulldozing kinds of passion. She learnt how to exploit that style to maximum effect in adaptations of two Tennessee Williams plays, *Cat on a Hot Tin Roof*, 1958, with Paul

OPPOSITE: studio portrait, 1953.
    Photographer Bud Fraker
ABOVE: *Conspirator*, 1949, with Robert Taylor
LEFT: *A Place in the Sun*, 1951, with
    Montgomery Clift

179

Newman, and opposite Clift again for *Suddenly, Last Summer*, 1959; she emerged Oscar nominated for both performances and near the top of the box office attractions.

Nevertheless, her acting never got more than grudging reviews, and it was said that the Oscar she won for *Butterfield 8*, 1960, was awarded out of sympathy for a serious dose of pneumonia. She certainly gave a mediocre performance in that film, but afterwards seemed to take herself more seriously. *Cleopatra*, 1963, was the beginning of her romance with Burton but the end of her days of un-selfconscious glory as the queen of classy but likeable trash. Taylor and Burton together seemed to inspire each other to ever-increasing heights of embarrassment, plodding wearily through fiascos like *The Sandpiper*, 1965, and *The Comedians*, 1967. *Reflections in a Golden Eye*, 1967, was only saved by the substitution for Burton of Brando. Burton and Taylor were good value, however, in theatrical screaming matches like *Who's Afraid of Virginia Woolf?*, 1966, for which Taylor won an Oscar, and *The Taming of the Shrew*, 1967, which had a redeeming sense of humour.

In the final analysis Taylor has transcended her screen career to become a kind of *paparazzi* version of Helen of Troy. She has joined that select band of media figures like Monroe and Jackie Onassis whose souls have been sucked from them by the flash, bang and wallop of a million flashbulbs.

ABOVE: off set *The Girl Who Had Everything*, 1953
RIGHT: *Cat on a Hot Tin Roof*, 1958, with Paul Newman
OPPOSITE: *The V.I.P.s*, 1963, with Richard Burton

JAYNE MANSFIELD

She resembles the ghost of Mae West hitched on to a souped-up fifties Cadillac, a triumph of artifice and engineering over nature, and a perfect parody of the aspirations of the American male as typified by the weedy Tony Randall: blonde, big busted, and with a giggly high-pitched whine he hopes his wife won't hear. Jayne Mansfield is easy to mock, but she always belonged to burlesque rather than straight drama, and deserves to be judged by her own standards. Those who identify vulgarity and bad taste with simple-mindedness have prevented her gaining any sort of critical respect for her two great masterpieces, *The Girl Can't Help It*, 1956, and *Will Success Spoil Rock Hunter?*, 1957, co-starring Tony Randall himself. She never took her sex-pot role as seriously as, for example, Monroe, in whose image she was supposed to be a kind of B-movie follow-up, and she never allowed herself or sex to be treated as more than a joke. Her idea of the body beautiful was like her second husband's, muscleman Mickey Hargitay, and the two satirized the fifties obsessions with perfection, abundance and luxury with their extravagant and parodic lifestyle. The only thing Mansfield took seriously was her ambition to become a star. But aside from Frank Tashlin, few directors understood how to use her to any advantage, and she began a slippery slide to oblivion in the early sixties that ended with her untimely death in a car crash on the way to a television engagement. She belonged to an era of plenty, and needed to be treated with a sort of exuberance that was quickly going out of fashion. A neon-pink Cadillac, a pair of pekinese, a heart-shaped swimming pool would be her mementoes, but not an Oscar.

LEFT: publicity portrait for *The Sheriff of Fractured Jaw*, 1958

Joan Collins is the great survivor. She was weaned in a show business family, studied at the Royal Academy of Dramatic Art for two years, and must have learned very early on how to 'give 'em all you've got'. But in gloomy post-war Britain poor Joan had to face the fact that sometimes even her best efforts were not always quite enough. She was a firm fixture in seedy black-and-white crime thrillers like *Cosh Boy*, 1952, as a moody Cockney tart, but she was always more *ersatz* Hollywood in her style, a kind of British Ava Gardner fed on austerity rations. But when she got to Hollywood, aged twenty-one, she seemed jinxed. If she couldn't tell the difference between bad movies and the real thing, audiences certainly could. She managed to turn up in the weakest films of Hollywood's top professionals: Howard Hawks probably wished he'd never bothered with *Land of the Pharaohs*, 1955, and Paul Newman should have felt the same way about *Rally 'Round the Flag, Boys!*, 1958. She was intelligent, good-looking, professional, enthusiastic, popular and talented; but somehow, when she started to act, she could never get it right. Even her second husband, Anthony Newley, involved her in a fiasco called *Can Heironymous Merkin . . . ?*, 1969 (after which they divorced). She never forgot how to act like a movie queen off screen, however. In her mid-forties, when most of her rivals had peaked or retired, she made a comeback in Britain in *The Stud*, 1978, and *The Bitch*, 1979. They were unashamedly tacky, but Joan worked away at her high-camp style and superbitch image so successfully that her role in the soap opera 'Dynasty' could have been made for her. Now at the peak of her popularity and in the height of fashion, she is still unmistakably reminiscent of that fifties penchant for fake leopard skin.

RIGHT: studio portrait, 1956.
Photographer Frank Powolny

AUDREY HEPBURN

With her doe-eyed charm and petite figure, Audrey Hepburn was a startlingly novel kind of beauty for the early fifties. Instead of buxom, blonde and giggling, she was slender, boyish and modest, with a *naïveté* which did not rule out sophistication. She became the first *gamine* to be accepted as overpoweringly chic, and opened up a niche later occupied by figures as diverse as Jean Seberg and Twiggy. It wasn't that Hepburn was a brilliant actress, or possessed a forceful personality. It was more that when the camera caught her face in close-up, everyone held their breath: she was simply so photogenic that everyone fell in love with her.

Ballet-trained, a model and bit-part movie actress, Hepburn was filming in the South of France when she met the great writer Colette. It was Colette who offered her the title role in the Broadway adaptation of her novel 'Gigi'; and from this Hepburn walked into *Roman Holiday*, 1953, as the young princess with whom Gregory Peck falls in love. She won an Academy Award for her role, proving to those who doubted that Hollywood could still be moved by novelty and freshness. She won another nomination for her next role in Billy Wilder's *Sabrina*, 1954, with Bogart and William Holden, and then played Natasha in King Vidor's ambitious *War and Peace*, 1956, opposite her new husband, Mel Ferrer. But it was *Funny Face*, 1957,

which best defined her qualities. She played a young model groomed by Fred Astaire for stardom in Stanley Donen's stylish version of the Gershwin musical, and, from photographer Richard Avedon's credits sequence onwards, her appeal was clear. Hepburn did not have to act so much as *be*: her face could register emotion simply by a blank stare.

She continued to have hits, and *Breakfast at Tiffany's*, 1961, brought her yet more admirers; but she seemed to have lost the freshness

ABOVE: publicity portrait for *Sabrina*, 1954.
Photographer Bud Fraker
OPPOSITE: publicity portrait for *Funny Face*, 1957.
Photographer Richard Avedon

which had been so surprising eight years before. Her role as Eliza Doolittle in *My Fair Lady*, 1964, seemed to show her artistic dilemma. She was indeed fine as the guttersnipe taken in by Pygmalion (the elderly Rex Harrison); but she was chosen over Julie Andrews because she was a 'safe' box office bet, and the 'safeness' of her performances was becoming all too evident. After *Two for the Road*, 1966, and *Wait Until Dark*, 1967, produced by Ferrer, and with five Oscar nominations to her credit, Hepburn went into semi-retirement with her second husband, and left her vintage fifties portraits to speak for themselves.

RIGHT: studio portrait, c. 1954.
    Photographer Bud Fraker
BELOW: publicity portrait for *Breakfast at Tiffany's*, 1961, with George Peppard

Even as a young twenty-six-year-old actress in Jacques Becker's *Touchez Pas au grisbi*, 1954, Jeanne Moreau was in command of the qualities which were to make her famous. She possessed a magnetic sense of urgency which could veer violently between extremes of sullenness and joy, yet always strike with precision. Whether she was passionate or moody, generous or scornful, she found it easy to give a scene its keynote, and then build her character into the one audiences watched to the end. Her broad smile and transfixing stares were unforgettable: she had learned the secret of screen acting, how to reveal emotions in a simple look or gesture, long before she became a new wave star in Louis Malle's *L'Ascenseur pour l'échafaud/Lift to the Scaffold* and *Les Amants*, both 1958, when she was already thirty. She caught the mood of the times perfectly with her boldly contemptuous look, her scorn for bourgeois morals, and her ability to stand up to or even dominate her screen men. She became a by-word for a strand of director's cinema, and in this area she gave her strongest performances: alienated in Antonioni's *La Notte*, capricious in François Truffaut's *Jules et Jim*, both 1961, compulsive in Jacques Demy's *La Baie des anges*, angst-ridden in Orson Welles' *Le Procès/The Trial*, coquettish in Joseph Losey's *Eva*, all three 1962, and seductive in Luis Buñuel's *Le Journal d'une Femme de chambre/Diary of a Chambermaid*, 1964. These directors realized how rare Moreau was: a figure loved by the camera, her face a rich canvas for both subtle and overpowering emotions, her skill and her talent strong enough to enable her to hang on to her integrity throughout her career.

ABOVE: *Touchez Pas au grisbi*, 1954, with Lino Ventura

BRIGITTE BARDOT

Brigitte Bardot was the Lolita who conquered the world, a pouting teenager, half-child and half-woman, whose very initials came to stand for a sexual myth: 'la bébé'. She was a uniquely French creation, able to mix a talent for scandal with a knowing *naïveté*, and under the careful eyes of her first husband and lifelong friend Roger Vadim, she was guided towards international stardom as the incarnation of sexual freedom. She had graduated from secondary parts to leads by 1955, but Vadim's first film as director, *Et Dieu créa la femme . . ., 1956*, launched her throughout the world, netting $4,000,000 in box office receipts on the way. She became a public figure, a bikini-clad *Liberté* arousing drowsy French men and women to frolic in the waters of St Tropez like oversexed children. B.B. was an instant cult, fuelled by the photographs of the *paparazzi* who pursued her, and by scenes like her shameless seduction of Jean Gabin in *En cas de malheur*, 1958. The basis of her appeal was not her acting but rather a protracted promise of striptease, that never failed to titillate her public even as far on as *Viva Maria*, 1965. She had little of that saving distance that a Dietrich might seek to retain. Her effect was blinding, dazzling, exciting, like that of her true medium, publicity; but unlike that medium, Bardot has worn well and can still corner headlines in the international press. As an actress, only in Jean-Luc Godard's *Le Mépris/ Contempt*, 1963, was she used with intelligence, and she gave perhaps her best performance as a movie star dazed at the confusion between her real life and the fake world of the movies, of which her bleached blonde hair was the constant reminder.

OPPOSITE: studio portrait, 1957
ABOVE: publicity portrait for *Doctor at Sea*, 1955
LEFT: *Et Dieu créa la femme . . .*, 1956, with Jean-Louis Trintignant

CLAUDIA CARDINALE

After B.B. came . . . C.C. Claudia Cardinale was projected as the Italian answer to Brigitte Bardot, a follow-up to Loren and Lollobrigida in true beauty-queen style. She had, it was true, those limpid eyes and statuesque figure which made physical attraction her most obvious asset. But after studying drama and marrying producer Franco Cristaldi, she was to star in a run of movies that included more than a handful of masterpieces. Visconti used her intelligently in his downbeat epic, *Rocco e i suoi Fratelli/Rocco and his Brothers*, 1960, while Fellini's *8½*, 1963, was the first of three successes in that year. Out of these, her best role was as the *nouvelle riche* with a vulgar laugh opposite Alain Delon in Visconti's *Il Gattopardo/The Leopard*, but she also managed to squeeze in her first Hollywood performance in *The Pink Panther*. While her Italian films had demanded more of her than her looks, the Hollywood style reduced her to a cipher – although *The Professionals*, 1966, was a fine exception. Her great advantage was that, although she was not in the first rank of actresses, she had learned one secret: how not to overact. She also possessed a fine instinct for choosing parts in films which were destined for greatness. The best example is her pivotal role in Sergio Leone's *C'era una Volta il West/Once Upon a Time in the West*, 1968, which gave her an operatic grandeur. Long after Bardot, Loren and Lollobrigida had ceased to care for cinema, she still respected the masters of her chosen medium, and has proved her commitment by continuing to make films in Italy, France, Britain and America.

LEFT: *La Ragazza di Bube*, 1963

When a young redhead rides into town following Frank Sinatra in *Some Came Running*, 1958, you notice her straight away. Shirley Maclaine shared her appealing lost-kitten look with her younger brother Warren Beatty, but her gorgeous mop of hair, generous smile, and kooky self-effacing nervousness made her a surer talent for comic pathos than any other Hollywood actress. She possessed a rare ability to let an audience in on her own bizarre world of personal logic within a few seconds of screen time, and from that moment on she can be as unbeatable as Lombard. Her early screen work was in *Artists and Models*, 1955, with Jerry Lewis, Hitchcock's *The Trouble With Harry*, 1955, and the major female part in *Around the World in 80 Days*, 1956; but she was best with a hard-boiled plot to support her soft-centred instincts. Billy Wilder's *The Apartment*, 1960, had her as elevator girl Fran Kubelik, involved with boss Fred MacMurray but flustering and falling in love with little guy Jack Lemmon in a tale of big city life that is a satirical gem; it has fewer soft edges than the same team's *Irma La Douce*, 1963, but by then MacLaine's portrayal of a tart with a heart of gold had had rather too many outings and was wearing thin. MacLaine and Lemmon were an ideal pair for bamboozling one another, both with an energetic flair for making the other seem a screwball. MacLaine's talent has another side to it, as the all-singing, all-dancing musical phenomenon of *Sweet Charity*, 1968. In later mawkish roles like *The Turning Point*, 1977, and *Terms of Endearment*, 1983, she appears to have matured in a less endearing manner than one might have expected: her comment 'I deserved it' after winning her 1984 Oscar leaves little doubt that self-effacing nervousness is no longer a problem.

RIGHT: studio portrait, 1958.
        Photographer Virgil Apger

LESLIE CARON

Leslie Caron made an enviable debut opposite Gene Kelly in MGM's *An American in Paris*, 1951, a role for which Kelly had personally chosen her after seeing her as a sixteen-year-old ballet dancer on the Paris stage four years before. Her bold features, large mouth and general cuteness marked her as suitable fodder of Hollywood stereotyping. She won an Oscar nomination for her role as a French waif in *Lili*, 1953, and must have had to grit her teeth to play the Cinderella role in *The Glass Slipper*, 1955, or even the young girl who falls in love with Fred Astaire in *Daddy Long Legs*, 1955. It was apparent that inside this charming Parisian waif there was an ambitious actress trying to get out; but she remained locked into the role of stylish first reserve for Audrey Hepburn. She later regarded her acceptance of the starring role in *Gigi*, 1958, as a bad mistake, for it typecast her as the charming Parisian *demoiselle*. Hepburn had herself turned the role down, despite her success in the stage version. It is certainly true that it was Caron's ironic misfortune to take plum roles in the decade's two leading Minnelli musicals, *An American in Paris* and *Gigi*, for after that her earnest attempt at kitchen-sink drama, in the British-made *The L-Shaped Room*, 1962, married ill with the public's image of her. She was only to dent that all-too-persistent image when she reappeared in her middle forties in *Sérail*, 1976, François Truffaut's *L'Homme qui amait les femmes/The Man Who Loved Women*, 1977, and, regrettably, in Ken Russell's *Valentino*, 1977. By then she was a long way indeed from Maurice Chevalier singing 'Zank 'eavens for leetle girls'.

LEFT: publicity portrait for *Gaby*, 1956

From the moment she appears in *A bout de souffle*, 1960, Jean Seberg makes a totally original impression. She wanders down a Parisian boulevard selling the New York 'Herald Tribune', looking the epitome of a kooky Francophile beatnik. Her hair is cropped, her clothes are cool, her glasses are dark, and she manages to project a mood which is both diffident and impetuous. She seemed a very modern kind of woman, and perfectly cast as the figurehead for Jean-Luc Godard's new style of cinema: abrupt, direct, able to change in both tone and style when mood dictates. Opposite Jean-Paul Belmondo she is like a willowy tree being caressed by a bear.

Seberg's role in the forefront of the 'new wave' was quite unexpected. This small-town girl from Iowa rose to international fame immediately after being selected to play the title part of *Saint Joan*, 1957, for Otto Preminger. Despite a critical panning she returned to the same director for the lead in *Bonjour tristesse*, 1958, in which she effectively projected a spoiled and capricious side to the character. But these and her later American roles, with the honourable exception of *Lilith*, 1964, seemed to run contrary to her own instinctive talent for earthbound *naïveté*. She had a guileless face, and her temperament did not seem to suit the American preference for 'technique'. She settled in France where her career progressed in fits and starts, but was at least set on course. Her suicide in 1979 was the culmination of many unhappy episodes, including a political smear campaign orchestrated against her by the CIA in the sixties.

ABOVE: *A bout de souffle*, 1960, with Jean-Paul Belmondo

193

URSULA ANDRESS

MONICA VITTI

Her impassive features stare out at audiences in no less than four films by director Michelangelo Antonioni, but somehow Monica Vitti managed to escape identification with the urban *ennui* so emphatically stated in *L'Avventura*, 1960, *La Notte*, 1961, *L'Eclisse*, 1962, and *Il Deserto rosso/ The Red Desert*, 1964. She was *the* face of a new style of existential cinema, possessing a screen image that seemed to resemble a painting of great beauty and meaning set down amidst the clutter and chaos of daily life. She later appeared in a series of comedies, Joseph Losey's 'swinging' *Modesty Blaise*, 1966, among them, but her forced zaniness vindicated Antonioni's miminalist and alienating approach to her screen persona.

BELOW: *L'Avventura*, 1960, with Gabriele Ferzetti

The Swiss-born Ursula Andress was the sort of girl who appealed to the James Bond in men. She was aloof, imperious, nonchalantly glamorous, and seemed to exist in a fantasy world of white bikinis, Caribbean beaches and Aston-Martins. When she arose from the sea in *Dr No*, 1962, most men probably thought she lived down there, donning her bikini only for visits to dry land. They must have been perplexed by her low-cut toga in *She*, 1965. As the former wife of John Derek, she seems with hindsight a forerunner of his later protégé, Bo. Andress survived disasters like *What's New Pussycat?*, 1965, and *Casino Royale*, 1967, to end up as a guest-star glamourpuss in international productions destined for oblivion.

ABOVE: publicity portrait for *She*, 1965

194

Perhaps because of her coolness, Stéphane Audran has always appeared an actress in the 'grand style'. Usually remote with a calm façade, her great interest on screen has proved to lie in detecting that façade begin to crumble. The ability to give away small clues to cracks in an impermeable exterior fits in absolutely with the driving force behind her films for director and one-time husband Claude Chabrol. She has become the constant Hitchcockian female in a French setting, her iciness usually a social rather than a purely personal attribute; for Chabrol is less democratic than Hitchcock, and

Audran is primarily a representative of the frozen caste of the bourgeoisie. After *Les Cousins* in 1959 she played a succession of minor roles, and married Chabrol in 1964; but only with *Les Biches*, 1968, did she really break through with a rounded performance as a lesbian involved in a complex web of emotional blackmail. *La Femme infidèle*, 1969, and *La Rupture*, 1970, saw an increased awareness of her abilities and of her own beauty, while *Le Boucher*, 1970, remains a landmark for her, with a chilling portrait of a provincial schoolteacher menaced by a local killer. Her sharp blue eyes are

appositely described as piercing, and as if to prove it her role in *Violette Nozière*, 1978, showed an aptitude for hatred surprising even to admirers of her previously embittered roles. She conjured up elegant smiles as a highly sexed wife in *Le Charme discret de la bourgeoisie*, 1972, and that performance stands as effective testimony to the healthy irony she injects into even her most villainous characters.

ABOVE: *La Femme infidèle*, 1969

MODERN TIMES

When Marilyn Monroe died in 1962, the time was ripe for the modern era to begin. Monroe had been the last of the true studio stars, raised and nourished on the Hollywood dreams which had so influenced her generation. Her life itself had spanned the movies' historical golden age. When she was born in 1926, Swanson was still at the height of her fame, and *The Jazz Singer* was just going into production; she grew up in the 1930s and 1940s as Jean Harlow and Lana Turner carved out their niches as blonde bombshells; and she died as the last incarnation of the old Hollywood system, rebelling in a confused way against her typecasting which would anyway have quickly become an intriguing anachronism. By the way she lived and the way she died, Monroe established two contradictory norms for the modern era. Firstly, the time when actresses would permit themselves to be rigidly bound by Hollywood conventions of stardom, behaviour, and servile femininity was over. And secondly, by the very brightness of this shooting star's fall from the heavens a new creature was born, a twin-headed monster of nostalgia and necrophilia that was to rake over Hollywood's embers and adopt an open-house attitude to its past glories.

In the careers of two contemporary stars like Meryl Streep and Bo Derek, both norms can be traced. Streep, born in 1951, grew up in the mid- to late sixties, during a convulsive period of social change in America. The unrest about the Vietnam War, the growing confidence of the youth movement, the inroads made by women's liberation and the intellectual acceptance of feminism all affected deeply entrenched attitudes. Streep herself inherited the legacy of this in the 1970s, after an orthodoxly conformist beginning at Vassar, Dartmouth, at the Yale Drama School, and on the Broadway stage. Her movies – like *Julia*, 1977, *Kramer vs Kramer*, 1979, *Sophie's Choice*, 1982, *Silkwood*, 1983, and most acutely *The French Lieutenant's Woman*, 1981 – reflect a thematic preoccupation: how to break loose from the past, from traditional patterns of female behaviour. She herself exemplifies a modern attitude to the cinema. She is earnest, theatrical, professional, self-consciously absorbed in technique, and able to draw on the achievements of the Actors' Studio pioneers. She is not owned, guided or dictated to by a Harry Cohn or Jack Warner, and she is allowed to live a quiet private life comforted by the vast financial rewards which do still attend the labours of a Hollywood star actress.

Bo Derek, born in 1955 and emerging during the same years as Streep, seems a throwback to a previous era. Promoted by her husband John Derek as the ideal dream girl of *10*, 1979, she rode on an international wave of publicity to become a new sex symbol. The idea was hardly novel, but Derek captured media attention as successfully as had William Fox and his promotion of Theda Bara (in jewels and veils instead of braids and a bikini) back in 1914. John Derek had already seen his second wife, Ursula Andress, arise from the waves in *Dr No*, 1962, to become a star, and was acute enough to recognize that an old trick was at least a tried and tested one. In newspapers, magazines and television chat shows, Bo Derek became a phenomenon strong enough to survive at least *Tarzan, the Ape Man*, 1981, if not *Bolero*, 1984.

While these stars climbed their respective ladders, the movie industry itself was coming to terms with adulthood. The slow fade-out of the Hollywood contract system, which had started in the fifties and accelerated in the early sixties, was over by the end of the decade. An hysterical response to the unexpected success of the low-budget, youth-orientated, pop-filled *Easy Rider*, 1969, proved that the old Hollywood structure had long been out of touch with changing social attitudes. Television, the international successes of pop groups like The Beatles, and the decline in the sheer amount of new movies, had all usurped cinema's centrality. The rewards were still there, but to be distributed among many media. Cinema audiences were increasingly seen in factions, and while the 'young' were probably worth targeting, the 'old' were not. Only long-awaited block-busters like *The Godfather*, 1972, or *Jaws*, 1975 brought them together. Similarly, actors' performances and scripts were attuned to what were assumed to be the codes of teenagers, or whichever portion of the population was targeted, as with *Saturday Night Fever*, 1977, or *Grease*, 1978. The role of the studio executive was transformed into that of a middleman; power de-volved to independent producers, stars and agents and a studio's contract players were no more.

Such general trends in the industry's overall structure concealed a more complex change. In the twenties, thirties and forties, studios hired actresses as types on a rigid and severe industrial production line. The many movies with a Garbo, a Bette Davis, a Joan Crawford or a Marlene Dietrich provided variations on a personality or a role in which the actresses were deemed to specialize. The emblematic, cartoon-like roles of the sweetheart and the vamp had grown more sophisti-cated, but cast a long shadow in influence. The formula for a Garbo movie, a Dietrich epic or a Bette Davis vehicle was immediately recognizable, and a crucial hook for a vast audience. By the sixties and seventies, that structure had all but vanished. Despite the rise of heroic types like Jill Clayburgh, Ellen Burstyn, Jane Fonda or Karen Black, or of comediennes like Goldie Hawn, actresses were no longer expected to remain consistent to a single type or role. Diane Keaton, Sissy Spacek, Faye Dunaway, even newcomers like Kathleen Turner, Rosanna Arquette, Debra Winger or Greta Scacchi, are more chameleon-like than their pre-decessors. The attitude towards typecasting has reversed. Once it was a positive achievement, a strong factor in audience recognition and identification; now it is a real drawback.

Other parts of the entertainment industry have mean-while adopted typecasting with glee. With the cinema now producing less, and with independent negotiation of contracts contributing to a diminution of daily in-terest, television and pop music have rushed in to fill the gap. The ballyhoo which used to greet a Bette Davis movie and cause Hedda Hopper's gossip column to bristle is now devoted to television's 'Dynasty', to Joan Collins and Linda Evans; soap opera aspires to be the opiate of the masses, and 'Dallas' and 'Dynasty' replay the scenarios of *Written On the Wind*, 1956, or *Mildred Pierce*, 1945, while Joan Crawford turns in her grave. The animated presence of Dolly Parton in mainstream music derives strength from her Hollywood-style pro-jection of body and soul; and in rock music, Madonna aims to become a Marilyn Monroe for the eighties, while Tina Turner has settled into a kind of vampish bitch-goddess role which is truly larger than life. Parton, Madonna and Turner have all made an impact in feature films (in *Nine to Five*, 1980, *Desperately Seek-ing Susan*, 1985, and *Mad Max III*, 1985, respectively), and seem likely to continue their movie careers: thus the cinema capitalizes on strong reputations made elsewhere, but has lost much of its power to establish new sexual icons.

The old ghosts have not been laid to rest. The arche-types and stereotypes which were created back in the twenties, thirties and forties now appear with increas-ing regularity not in the cinema, but in pop music, tele-vision, video clips, in a barrage of images which is diverse, fluid and relentless, but more restricted than cinema ever was. Audiences who are oblivious to Jean Harlow, Rita Hayworth or Ann Sheridan now rediscover their likenesses day in and day out. A show like 'Dallas' or 'Dynasty' has an abundance of plot, but little actual change of narrative or range of mood, while video clips pack into three minutes the ever-simplified iconography of comic-strip and cartoons, overlaid by a Hollywood glossy finish. The era's newest leading ladies, like their earliest prototypes, are mostly silent and un-named: they are the fleeting stars known only as David Bowie's *Blue Jean* or *Absolute Beginners* girl, Billy Joel's *Uptown Girl* or the selection of *Girls on Film* issued by Duran Duran, The Cars, Mick Jagger or Robert Palmer. These are now the items scanned by film producers and agents for new screen presences, but there is no guarantee of stardom or leading roles. There are few rules and few standards, nor much hope of maturing to more than flavour-of-the-month. The only rule of thumb is to adopt and adapt the archetypes – but with a sense of humour, irony or distance. It is a style typically known as post-modernist in other media, and regarded as an essentially pragmatic attitude that combines contra-dictory qualities in a quirky and unpredictable manner. With real talent, an actress can still rise above the prevailing trend. Kathleen Turner and Rosanna Arquette are, for example, in demand simply by virtue of their flexibility and range. As for the future, not even their agents would confidently predict the outcome.

JANE FONDA

There have been at least four Jane Fondas. There was a timid starlet in *The Chapman Report*, 1962, who grew into the space-fantasy sex-kitten of *Barbarella*, 1968; then the pro-Vietcong outspoken media figure of *Tout va bien*, 1972, was supplanted by the confident Hollywood actress. Since her Oscar nomination for *They Shoot Horses Don't They?*, 1969, and her Best Actress award for *Klute*, 1971, right up to *The China Syndrome*, 1979, and *Nine to Five*, 1980, Fonda has reassured doubters – including herself – that there is still a chance to express modern feminist attitudes in a hidebound, male-dominated industry. Personally she has had a major triumph. The daughter of Henry Fonda, one-time wife of Roger Vadim, and well-known anti-establishment figure, she has managed to hijack the leadership of Hollywood's grand tradition of leading ladies and drag it into modern times. She fought for adult and mature roles concerning sensitive social issues in movies like *Julia*, 1977, *Coming Home*, 1978, *The Electric Horseman*, 1979, and *The China Syndrome*. And she has earned in her own right a widespread popularity all the more surprising after her public vilification in the sixties and seventies. But she can show her Hollywood weaknesses as well as her strengths. She is earnest but corny, comic but sentimental, passionate yet superficial; she can make an audience curl up in embarrassment moments after making them yell out hurrahs. *On Golden Pond*, 1981, allowed her an on-screen reconciliation with both her father and with the old Hollywood tradition in which she is rooted. She is the grandest 'inside outsider' of the film business, and has had to fight out her rebellion in the uncomfortable glare of the public; that alone has given her a perversely unique status.

LEFT: publicity portrait for *Cat Ballou*, 1965
OPPOSITE ABOVE: *Walk On the Wild Side*, 1962, with Laurence Harvey
OPPOSITE BELOW: *Julia*, 1977

VANESSA REDGRAVE

For all her undoubted ability as an actress, Vanessa Redgrave has persisted in choosing movie roles with the inspiration of someone blindfolded and wielding a pin. Even if her Oscar-winning role in *Julia*, 1977, made audiences weep, if her sylph-like beauty in *Camelot*, 1967, caused hearts to melt, or if *Yanks*, 1979, proved her effortless ease in screen acting, there are more than enough horrors in her career to make an intelligent audience shake its head at the wasted opportunity. Can the woman who played Anne Boleyn in *A Man For All Seasons*, 1966, take seriously the starring part in Ken Russell's shamelessly crude version of *The Devils*,

1971? Are there not less cynical ways of paying rent or raising political funds than by taking prominent roles in the likes of *Murder on the Orient Express*, 1974, *Mary, Queen of Scots*, 1971, and *Bear Island*, 1979? She has a tendency towards earnestness and pretension that made her perfect for *Isadora*, 1968, and her other best roles remain those in *Morgan – A Suitable Case for Treatment*, and *Blow-Up*, both 1966. In *Morgan* she showed a flair for surreal comedy which has since remained unexplored, while Antonioni's abstract detective story in swinging London used her as an intriguingly contemporary heroine. Since then she seems to have concentrated

on costume dramas such as *Agatha*, 1979, in which her theatrical training is generally only used as a snobbish mannerism. She has avoided modern-day acting roles, except under her own name as a real-life modern revolutionary, so *Wetherby*, 1985, was a welcome change. As a schoolteacher in a remote Yorkshire village, she took on her best role in years and proved that on the right night she can outclass almost anyone on screen.

ABOVE: *Camelot*, 1967

Barbra Streisand is above all a performer. She possesses a near-perfect instinct for knockout showbiz schmaltz – but with a tendency to deliver a powerhouse punch where a more skilful cinema actress might achieve more with less. She started out as a singer with a driving ambition to act, and made her name on Broadway in 1962. Her first movie was as the kooky ugly duckling Fanny Brice in *Funny Girl*, 1968, an enormously successful movie that established this gawky twenty-six-year old as a serious superstar with an Oscar under her belt and a contract with CBS that would produce a clutch of million-selling records. Nevertheless her follow-up in *Hello, Dolly!*, 1969, was not successful, and *On a Clear Day You Can See Forever*, 1970, with Yves Montand, met a similar fate. *The Owl and the Pussycat*, 1970, and the Peter Bogdanovich comedy *What's Up Doc?*, 1972, showed a nascent talent for screwball craziness; *The Way We Were*, 1973, proved how sensitive she could get with Robert Redford, but *A Star Is Born*, 1976, and *The Main Event*, 1979, proved ear-thumping, eye-straining exercises in megalomania, although commercial successes for all that. Her ambitions triumphed when she wrote, directed, produced and starred in *Yentl*, 1983, but her crass sentimentalization of Isaac Bashevis Singer's story was ultimately unappealing, little more than a tearful wallow. Now only in her mid-forties (and divorced from Elliott Gould), she is a sort of Sarah Bernhardt of Hollywood, demanding attention for her own charisma with all the cultivated arrogance of a pop Brooklyn diva. No matter how multi-talented, she seems increasingly remote from contemporary concerns, as if show business provides all her questions and all her answers; and she fails to win fans among audiences who don't relish being yelled at in the stalls.

RIGHT: *Funny Girl*, 1968

JULIE CHRISTIE

From the moment Julie Christie appeared as Tom Courtenay's dream girl in *Billy Liar*, 1963, she was seized on as the very epitome of the swinging sixties. Pushed through the acerbic fashion world of *Darling*, 1965, she emerged with an Oscar, as many American fans as the Beatles, and the successful contender for the Scarlett O'Hara role of the decade as Lara in *Doctor Zhivago*, 1965. She was beautiful without make-up, vivacious yet vulnerable, but had such an unaffected air it suggested her whole rise to fame was as much a surprise to her as to anybody else. She was deemed to have 'It', and thus defined the sixties as neatly as Clara Bow had symbolized the flappers of the twenties – yet she seemed to long to be 'without it'. She veered towards the arty side of commercial cinema for François Truffaut in *Fahrenheit 451*, 1966, and in *Far From the Madding Crowd*, 1967; and she was very much on form for the then off-form directors Joseph Losey and Robert Altman, in *The Go-Between* and *McCabe and Mrs Miller*, both 1971. (She was nominated for an Oscar for the latter.) *Don't Look Now*, 1973, caught her in the unfamiliar world of an erotically chilling thriller. By the time of *Shampoo*, 1975, and *Heaven Can Wait*, 1978, she had graduated to the Californian 'me'-centred world of Warren Beatty and seemed to be wondering whether these painstakingly light comedies were worth all the effort. Her answer was to turn down subsequent Hollywood offers in favour of roles that touched her conscience and her politics, such as the leads in *Memoirs of a Survivor*, 1981, *The Return of the Soldier*, 1982, and *Heat and Dust*, 1983, from novels by Doris Lessing, Rebecca West and Ruth Prawer Jhabvala respectively. More so than her American counterpart Jane Fonda, she seems to have decided that the movies hold little satisfaction for her.

LEFT: *Darling*, 1965
OPPOSITE: *The Go-Between*, 1971

Even if she was born twenty years too late to cultivate it, Catherine Deneuve was the very embodiment of the Hitch-cockian ice-cold blonde, and a potentially more rewarding model than Kim Novak, Tippi Hedren or even Grace Kelly. Her role for Roman Polanski as the ill-fated heroine of *Repulsion*, 1965, showed that someone had indeed noticed her peculiarly frigid quality and her capacity for a razor's edge display of terror. It was an unlikely advance, however, for an actress who had started a career under the influence of Roger Vadim, and then made her name in Jacques Demy's colourful musical *Les Parapluies de Cherbourg*, 1964. She followed that success with a starring role, with her sister Françoise Dorléac, in Demy's *Les Demoiselles de Rochefort*, 1967; and in the same year she made Luis Buñuel's *Belle de Jour*. As the elegant Parisian housewife whose sexual fantasies lead her into part-time prostitution, Deneuve gave a definitive portrayal of a character whose calm surface belies seething depths of unpredictable passions. Her performance in Buñuel's *Tristana*, 1970, was similarly gripping, managing to create an atmosphere of stifling repression and crippled beauty; but although her roles persistently gained in stature during the seventies, and she became France's undisputed leading star, Truffaut's *Le Dernier Métro*, 1980, was a rare exploitation of her real abilities. Today she is thought of like some expensive perfume, but her image seems to contradict and trivialize her capacity as an actress. For despite two resolutely modern roles in *Repulsion* and *Belle de Jour*, and despite having consorted with such symbols of sixties modernity as Vadim, Marcello Mastroianni and photographer David Bailey, she remains an essentially conservative figure, orthodox and undissenting.

OPPOSITE: *Belle de Jour*, 1967, with Jean Sorel
RIGHT: *The Hunger*, 1983

MIA FARROW

DIANE KEATON

Despite her well-publicized private life – which includes marriages to Frank Sinatra and André Previn, and a romance with Woody Allen – Mia Farrow manages to convince with almost every performance that she is a fresh-faced naïve. Perhaps it is her wide-eyed, freckled face that makes her peculiarly suitable for such epics of urban sinfulness as Roman Polanski's *Rosemary's Baby*, 1968, and *John and Mary*, 1969. She retains her frail charm even when laden down with costume in *The Great Gatsby*, 1974; and in her films with Woody Allen it was decidedly reasserted, from *A Midsummer Night's Sex Comedy*, 1982, through *Zelig*, 1983, to her radiant brilliance in *Broadway Danny Rose*, 1984, *The Purple Rose of Cairo*, 1985, and *Hannah and Her Sisters*, 1986.

BELOW: *The Great Gatsby*, 1974

From playing Woody Allen's favourite kook, to conjuring the heavy emotion of *Shoot the Moon*, 1982, Diane Keaton has, for many, never ceased to be *Annie Hall*, 1977, a role for which she won a Best Actress Oscar. She has a bizarre West Coast vagueness which was the ideal attribute for co-starring opposite the nervy, articulate New Yorker Woody Allen in *Play It Again Sam*, 1972, through to *Manhattan*, 1979. Even so, her dramatic roles in *Interiors*, 1978, *Looking for Mr Goodbar*, 1977, and *Mrs Soffel*, 1984, leave a sense of overpowering vacancy, and if her sincerity in *Reds*, 1981, was clearly under strain, surprisingly nothing has yet managed to dent her personal popularity.

ABOVE: *Interiors*, 1978

OPPOSITE: *Bonnie and Clyde*, 1967

Just when you thought there could never be another Joan Crawford ... along comes Faye Dunaway. Her hysterically camp portrayal of a real-life Crawford in *Mommie Dearest*, 1981, seemed at first sight to be a calculated piece of Grand Guignol, a berserk overstatement of a larger-than-life character. But looking back you can't be so sure. For Dunaway's sense of melodrama, and of herself as the *grand dame* of the genre, may well have been nurturing itself over the years.

She didn't start out that way. For years after her Oscar-nominated performance with Warren Beatty in *Bonnie and Clyde*, 1967, she remained Bonnie Parker, the cigar-chewing, machine-gun toting Southern gal transformed into a soft-focus romantic out-

law. From there she drifted into *The Thomas Crown Affair*, 1968, a caper movie with Steve McQueen, and on into the adult entanglements of Elia Kazan's *The Arrangement*, 1969; but neither dispelled the rosy hue of *Bonnie*. It was not until Roman Polanski came along with *Chinatown*, 1974, that she found a part she could get her teeth into.

And how.... As Mrs Evelyn Mulwray, Dunaway was the poisonous heart of a plot which skids from *film noir* into the deep waters of family melodrama without the audience guessing. She starts as the object of detective Jack Nicholson's investigation, but ends by stealing his movie with a performance of intense emotional power, one which hints at Craw-

ford's eye-rolling frenzy and leaves the audience devastated.

Network, 1976, gave her both an Oscar and all the opportunities she needed to indulge in angry histrionics; after that Dunaway had to wait until *Mommie Dearest* to provide another true she-monster for her. Her interpretation of the *The Wicked Lady*, 1983, did not suggest that Dunaway wanted to change, but the time may yet come when she does.

ABOVE: *The Thomas Crown Affair*, 1968, with Steve McQueen
OPPOSITE: *The Arrangement*, 1969

SISSY SPACEK

You couldn't imagine a more unlikely heroine of the seventies than Sissy Spacek. Here was a twenty-four-year-old actress with freckles, wispy hair and a whispering voice playing a fifteen-year-old murderess in a muted art film called *Badlands*, 1973 – and doing it brilliantly. She was getting on for twenty-seven when she played a high-school girl terrorized by classmates in *Carrie*, 1976, and from that moment has graduated to more mature roles with an assuredness and confidence that in retrospect seem astonishing. Her training under Lee Strasberg at the Actor's Studio has stood her in good stead. She took a sidestep for Robert Altman's dramatic style in *Welcome to L.A.*, 1977, and *Three Women*, 1977, and went beatnik for *Heart Beat*, 1979; but with *Coal Miner's Daughter*, 1980, found a deserved place in the movie establishment and the public's heart. She won an Oscar for her portrayal of country singer Loretta Lynn, and was grimly effective in capturing her desperate determination to rise above her poverty and family torment. It was a classic tale of rags-to-riches, no different in design to a thirties melodrama; but Spacek endowed it with a contemporary freshness and proved her strength and flexibility. Her performance in *Raggedy Man*, 1981, directed by her husband Jack Fisk, could not quite lift it out of the doldrums; but in *Missing*, 1982, her impassioned straight-from-the-heart style of acting was truly gripping. *The River*, 1984, confirmed her as most popular when identified with the rural backwoods of America, to which her natural, fresh-faced prettiness is admirably suited.

LEFT: publicity portrait for *Three Women*, 1977

Jessica Lange must be the only Hollywood leading lady of recent times who had to look for a comeback after her first film. For *King Kong*, 1976, was so derisibly tacky that despite a seven-year contract to its producer Dino De Laurentiis, Lange did not make another appearance until *All That Jazz*, 1979 – and even then it was in a minor role. She followed that with yet another clinker called *How to Beat the High Cost of Living*, 1980, before finally getting it right with the Lana Turner role of Cora in the remake of *The Postman Always Rings Twice*, 1981, opposite Jack Nicholson. She took full advantage of this peach of a role, displaying an impetuous sexual yearning which had been noticeably absent in her previous movies. If her performance hinted that she was capable of overstatement, it was nothing compared to her title role as *Frances*, 1982, the sad story of the Hollywood actress Frances Farmer's struggle against mental instability. Lange was nominated for an Oscar for her full-tilt, hysterical portrayal of every last nuance of mental breakdown. It was pure soap opera; but it did push her to the top of the queue for an Oscar, which she won for a comic role opposite Dustin Hoffman's *Tootsie*, also 1982. Her rise to the show business aristocracy had already been announced by an early association with dancer Mikhail Baryshnikov, and her romance with America's most eligible man, Sam Shepard, only confirmed that status. It also produced a distinguished contribution, *Country*, 1984, to a new cycle of rural movies, even if she is generally more convincing in an urban role with glamorous fringes; and she was superb in – and Oscar nominated for – *Sweet Dreams*, 1985.

ABOVE: *The Postman Always Rings Twice*, 1981, with Jack Nicholson

HANNA SCHYGULLA

When Hanna Schygulla became an international star, the publicity for her film *Lili Marleen*, 1981, boasted that here was the new Dietrich. Both were certainly German; both certainly played cabaret performers in stockings, with Schygulla consciously posed like Lola Lola from *Der blaue Engel*; and Schygulla did appear to have her own mentor, *à la* Josef Von Sternberg, in director Rainer Werner Fassbinder, with whom she had made some fifteen movies in just over a decade. But for all that, Schygulla's persona was more a bitter mockery of Dietrich than an emulation of her. She had teamed up with Fassbinder at

drama school in Munich, and together they built up a practised company of actors. Schygulla produced a series of fine performances in *Die bitteren Tränen der Petra von Kant/The Bitter Tears of Petra von Kant*, 1972, *Effi Briest*, 1974, and the allegorical *Die Ehe der Maria Braun/The Marriage of Maria Braun*, 1978. But again, her interpretation of the symbolic character of the latter title was not admiring, it was bitter satire. The early nihilistic tendencies of student *anti-theater* showed through Schygulla's performances, and matured into an eerie ability to play unpleasant characters with unsettling sympathy. For herself, she

has scorned conventional ideas of stardom but has still found herself sought after by established directors like Jean-Luc Godard and Andrzej Wajda, and even by the makers of American television series. Whatever follows, she will always remain as the ill-fated Maria Braun, whose illicit liaisons and callous determination to succeed represent a character who stands for the whole post-war history of her country, a role Schygulla played with triumphant ease.

ABOVE: *Die Ehe der Maria Braun*, 1978

Isabelle Adjani has a singularly expressive face with cheeks of almost deathly pallor and eyes capable of a witheringly intense gaze, for she is the inspired mix of an Algerian–Turkish father and German mother, and raised in France. Adjani was already an actress in her teens, and her performances at the prestigious Comédie-Française in Paris brought acclaim as the most brilliant of her generation. When she left to go into the movies, and played the lead in François Truffaut's *L'Histoire d'Adèle H.*, 1975, at the age of twenty, the critics compared her to Jeanne Moreau, and she was nominated for an Oscar for the film. But her career since then has wavered, offering riveting performances but uncertain direction. It is difficult to tell exactly *what* she is thinking, although she usually suggests it is of some importance; hence her label 'enigmatic'. Roman Polanski used her in *Le Locataire/The Tenant*, 1976, and she was bleakly existentialist opposite a comfortably bland Ryan O'Neal in *The Driver*, 1978, with which she made her American debut. In Werner Herzog's *Nosferatu Phantom der Nacht*, 1978, her portrayal of Lucy was frighteningly anaemic but ultimately overpowered by Klaus Kinski's manic characterization, and she was better as a suitably romantic Emily in *Les Sœurs Brontë*, 1979. Although she often seems to be more at ease in her French films than in international productions, her performance in James Ivory's *Quartet*, 1981, won her a Best Actress award at Cannes; and the peculiar *Possession*, 1981, directed by Andrzej Zulawski, proved that she could hold her own admirably in the face of obsessional, psychotic nightmares. If this suggested it was time for a little light relief, that is exactly what she found in *Ishtar*, 1986, with Dustin Hoffman and Warren Beatty.

ABOVE: *Quartet*, 1981

SIGOURNEY WEAVER ISABELLE HUPPERT

As the meek and malleable heroine of *La Dentellière/The Lacemaker*, 1977, Isabelle Huppert's debut on the international scene was almost apologetic. Her own docile, freckled face seemed to capture so closely the character's restrained and tragic mood that she barely appeared to be acting; only with her role as the spiteful and bitter anti-heroine *Violette Nozière*, 1978, for Claude Chabrol was her range as an actress evident. Her selection for the Michael Cimino epic and spectacular flop *Heaven's Gate*, 1980, was a mixed blessing for her, and it was no surprise that she should return to France for *Sauve qui peut (la vie)/Slow Motion*, 1980, for Jean-Luc Godard. *Coup de torchon/Clean Slate* and *Passion*, both 1982, confirmed her as a bankable European star with little need for whatever Hollywood has to offer.

BELOW: portrait, 1980

Sigourney Weaver has it all: a first name plucked from 'The Great Gatsby', an M.A. from Yale Drama School, and those taut, chiselled looks so reminiscent of the Katharine Hepburn–Jane Fonda style. But she has yet to find the right leading role. She sparkled briefly with Mel Gibson in *The Year of Living Dangerously*, 1982, but her other male foils have ranged between a berserk New York spook in *Ghostbusters*, 1984, to a voyeuristic janitor in *Eyewitness*, 1981. She hit the cover of 'Newsweek' after starring opposite a slimy outer-space reptile in *Alien*, 1979. A latter-day Spencer Tracy is what she deserves, and *Half Moon Street*, 1986, has given her at least a chance of finding him.

ABOVE: portrait, 1984

OPPOSITE: publicity portrait for *Kramer vs Kramer*, 1979

Meryl Streep is a class act. She may not always be likeable. She may sometimes appear obsessively worthy, irritating, precious or theatrical. But it cannot be said she comes second on many lists of the best film actresses around. The worst that could be said is she seems to have too much taste for her own good. In a mere eight years since her first appearance in *Julia*, 1977, she has scarcely made a wrong move and has hogged the strongest parts around, from *Kramer vs Kramer*, 1979, to *The French Lieutenant's Woman*, 1981, *Sophie's Choice*, 1982, and *Silkwood*, 1983 – picking up a clutch of Oscars on the way. More

RIGHT: *Sophie's Choice*, 1982, with Kevin Kline
BELOW: *The French Lieutenant's Woman*, 1981, with Jeremy Irons

than that, she has carved out for herself a recognizable territory as a woman struggling with the problems of independence, which has confimed her position as a resolutely contemporary actress.

Much of this was obvious even from a 'man's movie' like *The Deer Hunter*, 1978, in which Streep plays the girlfriend back home. She entered politics as a calculating and ambitious assistant to a senator in *The Seduction of Joe Tynan*, 1979, but that self-centred ruthlessness was tempered by a more sympathetic role as the divorcée in *Kramer vs Kramer*, in which she successfully stood up to Dustin Hoffman's practised scene-stealing techniques with credit.

Kramer's status as the archetypal modern weepie, one which cunningly shifts time-honoured plotting tech-

niques on to the scattered relationships of the 1970s, also emphasized Streep's tendency to tears. It never takes much to make Streep weep, and she has indeed opted for melodrama with an almost masochistic passion. *The French Lieutenant's Woman* is an example, a somewhat broken-backed affair dipping unsatisfactorily between ancient and modern settings. Streep's taste for trauma led her to the television soap opera 'Holocaust', 1978, and to *Sophie's Choice*, and in award-winning performances she took on the suffering of the Jews under Nazism with tear-stained virtuosity. *Plenty*, 1985, offered her a solo turn in another English guise as a woman on the edge of a nervous breakdown.

Streep comes from a middle-class, New Jersey Dutch background, and studied at Yale's famous drama

school; forty plays over three years trained and sharpened her technique, and that classical, theatrical grounding is worn on her sleeve as evidence of her good taste and pedigree dramatic breeding. But Streep's cool crisp precision is something less sympathetic than, for example, Ingrid Bergman's warmth and generosity, and perhaps her least traumatic venture *Falling in Love*, 1984, opposite Robert De Niro was a recognition of this, and an attempt to remedy it. It didn't. But for the time being at least, Streep's name will continue to feature in the lists of Oscar nominations (in 1986 for *Out of Africa*), and everyone else will continue to play second fiddle.

ABOVE: *Plenty*, 1985

NASTASSJA KINSKI

For all the doubts about her acting, her seriousness, her ability or her taste Nastassja Kinski has always *looked* as if she should be a movie star. The estranged daughter of Werner Herzog's star Klaus Kinski, Nastassja was spotted aged fourteen dancing in a Munich nightclub by Wim Wenders' wife, and as a result was cast in a small role in that director's *Falsche Bewegung/Wrong Movement*, 1975. An acting course in New York at the Actor's Studio followed, then a year-long affair with Roman Polanski while still in her teens. The relationship brought him an unlikely heroine in *Tess*, 1979, and her an undisguised dislike of his directorial methods; but she did prove undeniably strong as Thomas Hardy's romantic character, despite a German twang to her Dorset accent. She seemed out of place in the happy-go-lucky fairy-tale atmosphere of Francis Ford Coppola's *One From the Heart*, 1982, for her alluring eyes seemed far more suited to the darker setting of a film like *Cat People*, 1982; but the formula still didn't work, for she seemed ill-matched with Malcolm McDowell, and each competed with the other with their sneering lip movements. Still photographs hint at the magic for which these films were striving; Kinski's young face expresses a youthful sensuality, while her eyes seem heavy-lidded with a sense of fate. She possesses the face of a child with an adult's knowledge. Kinski strolled through *La Lune dans le caniveau/The Moon in the Gutter*, 1983, as yet another alluring night-time nymph, but found her best role to date in Wenders' *Paris, Texas*, 1984. She played a symbolic role that, for once, achieved its intended effect, and at last Kinski produced a performance that lived up to her promise.

ABOVE: *Tess*, 1979
LEFT: *Paris, Texas*, 1984
OPPOSITE: *Cat People*, 1982

KATHLEEN TURNER

Kathleen Turner walked into Lawrence Kasdan's *Body Heat*, 1981, as an unknown, and made the part of the coolly erotic killer her own. Thus she took on the *film noir* ghosts of Barbara Stanwyck and Lauren Bacall and, against all odds, won. Here, everybody thought, was a real find, a *femme fatale* for the eighties. So she surprised even her own admirers when she turned up as a comic vamp opposite Steve Martin in the hilarious *The Man With Two Brains*, 1983; and then turned into a timid young novelist transported into a world of romantic adventure with Michael Douglas for *Romancing the Stone*, 1984. Nobody had anticipated such adaptability. But when *Crimes of Passion*, 1985, was released with Turner as China Blue, a night-time hooker and day-time fashion designer, it suddenly dawned that Turner wasn't just a find, she was an authentic screen actress with a range that was truly staggering. She proved that again in *Prizzi's Honour*, 1985, opposite Jack Nicholson. She effortlessly played out to the limits of black comedy as a devious Mafia hit-girl who conveniently falls in love with the hit-man who has to kill her; the challenge of scoring points off Nicholson was nothing compared to making her character believable. It is not surprising that she should have become a strong contender for the position of Hollywood's most versatile actress, and her follow-up with Michael Douglas in Lewis Teague's *The Jewel of the Nile*, 1986, has only increased her popularity. There hasn't been anybody quite like her for years.

LEFT: publicity portrait for *Body Heat*, 1981

Admirers of Debra Winger have been known to refer to her as a mythical Jewish American Princess swept up on to the big screen. It has always seemed a dubious compliment, but at least it suggests that the actress who once played Wonder Woman's kid sister on television has now graduated to better things. She has had some career doubts and some false starts, as her spell on a kibbutz and later studying sociology suggest. But having survived television and minor film roles in *Slumber Party '57*, 1976, and *Thank God It's Friday*, 1978, she set her sights on the big time. The first step was snatching the lead opposite John Travolta in *Urban Cowboy*, 1980, in which Winger memorably tamed a mechanical bull in a saloon as if it were second nature. Her moment of true glory came in *An Officer and a Gentleman*, 1982, for her love scenes with Richard Gere helped to make this military fairy-tale somehow believable and an unexpected smash hit; she received her reward with an Oscar nomination. And since no-one talks about her role in *Cannery Row*, 1982, because so few people saw it, it seemed that her second Oscar nomination for *Terms of Endearment*, 1983, followed hard on her first, and she was showered in gold dust. Her performance as a young daughter dying of cancer was one of which Irene Dunne would have been proud, and what audiences could see through a veil of streaming tears they pronounced splendid. Her versatility showed in *Mike's Murder*, 1984, but truly plum roles like her Oscar contenders may be few and far between.

RIGHT: *An Officer and a Gentleman*, 1982

ROSANNA ARQUETTE   MICHELLE PFEIFFER

When Rosanna Arquette was growing up as a child of the sixties she had pictures of Marilyn Monroe on her wall, but secretly wanted to be Natalie Wood. If Monroe was like an impossible dream, Wood's doe-eyed charm was something to aim for. Arquette showed tender toughness as Gary Gilmore's girlfriend in *The Executioner's Song*, 1982, and in *Baby, It's You*, 1983, and played the scatty housewife who is *Desperately Seeking Susan*, 1985. Arquette has a manic energy that earned her a role in Martin Scorsese's black comedy, *After Hours*, 1985, while her soulful expression was turned on for *Silverado*, 1985; suggesting that children of the eighties may one day want to grow up to be Rosanna Arquette.

BELOW: *The Executioner's Song*, 1982

Michelle Pfeiffer was sufficiently eye-catching in *Scarface*, 1983, as Al Pacino's moll, and sufficiently kooky opposite Jeff Goldblum in *Into the Night*, 1985, for all the old comparisons to be wheeled out. She was as cheeky as Harlow, as crazy as Lombard, as vivacious as Monroe or as icy as Grace Kelly, depending on who might be your favourite. Pfeiffer has that blank stare of the made-to-measure Californian blonde which suggests she lives as much in the present tense as do her audiences. Certainly she looked out of place in the medieval *Ladyhawke*, 1985, and even in the fifties revival, *Grease II*, only really seeming at home in the laid-back Los Angeles night-time. Cool, cute and suntanned, she's the embodiment of 'California über alles'.

ABOVE: *Ladyhawke*, 1985

Since her native British film industry remains a notorious black hole for aspiring movie actresses, Greta Scacchi has had to cast her net far and wide for good parts. Her impish good looks first attracted attention in James Ivory's Anglo-Indian production *Heat and Dust*, 1983; she plays an English wife who scandalizes her Raj friends by falling in love with an Indian. She surfaced again in *The Coca Cola Kid*, 1985, as an Australian radical opposite American Eric Roberts, in a film directed by the Yugoslav Dusan Makavejev. In between were strong roles on British television opposite Laurence Olivier in 'The Ebony Tower', 1984, and with James Mason and Alan Bates in 'Dr Fischer of Geneva', 1984; a leading role in the Australian television series 'Waterfront', 1983; and the title role of 'Camille', 1984, for American television. The British thriller *Defence of the Realm*, 1985, sadly underplayed her role as a Member of Parliament's secretary who is caught up in a spy scandal, but she survived long enough on screen to demonstrate that she is worthy of more than that. Scacchi is the daughter of an Italian painter and an Englishwoman, and it's been her fate to have to renew her passport and to suffer at the hands of one or two domineering directors and stars; but one day she should at last get her own back.

RIGHT: portrait, 1985.
Photographer Donald Cooper

INDEX

Adjani, Isabelle (b. 1955)	213	Goddard, Paulette (b. 1911)	92	Pickford, Mary (1893-1979)	21
Andress, Ursula (b. 1936)	194	Grahame, Gloria (1925-1981)	158		
Arletty (b. 1898)	128			Redgrave, Vanessa (b. 1937)	200
Arquette, Rosanna (b. 1959)	222	Harlow, Jean (1911-1937)	50	Rogers, Ginger (b. 1911)	89
Arthur, Jean (b. 1908)	55	Hayward, Susan (1918-1975)	140	Russell, Jane (b. 1921)	154
Astor, Mary (b. 1906)	48	Hayworth, Rita (b. 1918)	141	Russell, Rosalind (1908-1976)	77
Audran, Stéphane (b. 1932)	195	Hepburn, Audrey (b. 1929)	184		
		Hepburn, Katharine (b. 1907)	83	Scacchi, Greta (b. 1960)	223
Bacall, Lauren (b. 1924)	136	Hopkins, Miriam (1902-1972)	48	Schygulla, Hanna (b. 1943)	212
Bankhead, Tallulah (1902-1968)	44	Huppert, Isabelle (b. 1956)	214	Seberg, Jean (1938-1979)	193
Bara, Theda (1890-1955)	14			Shearer, Norma (1900-1983)	40
Bardot, Brigitte (b. 1934)	188	Jones, Jennifer (b. 1919)	139	Sheridan, Ann (1915-1967)	131
Bennett, Constance (1904-1965)	78			Sidney, Sylvia (b. 1910)	54
Bennett, Joan (b. 1910)	79	Keaton, Diane (b. 1946)	206	Signoret, Simone (1921-1985)	174
Bergman, Ingrid (1915-1982)	119	Kelly, Grace (1928-1982)	160	Simmons, Jean (b. 1929)	176
Bow, Clara (1905-1965)	26	Kendall, Kay (1926-1959)	156	Simon, Simone (b. 1914)	126
Brent, Evelyn (1899-1975)	16	Kerr, Deborah (b. 1921)	146	Spacek, Sissy (b. 1949)	210
Brooks, Louise (1906-1985)	23	Kinski, Nastassja (b. 1961)	218	Stanwyck, Barbara (b. 1907)	110
				Streep, Meryl (b. 1951)	215
Cardinale, Claudia (b. 1939)	192	Lake, Veronica (1919-1973)	118	Streisand, Barbra (b. 1942)	201
Caron, Leslie (b. 1931)	190	Lamarr, Hedy (b. 1913)	93	Swanson, Gloria (1899-1983)	29
Carroll, Madeleine (b. 1906)	49	Lamour, Dorothy (b. 1914)	82		
Charisse, Cyd (b. 1921)	155	Lange, Jessica (b. 1950)	211	Taylor, Elizabeth (b. 1932)	178
Christie, Julie (b. 1941)	202	Leigh, Janet (b. 1927)	159	Tierney, Gene (b. 1920)	114
Colbert, Claudette (b. 1905)	62	Leigh, Vivien (1913-1967)	104	Turner, Kathleen (b. 1954)	220
Collins, Joan (b. 1933)	183	Lockwood, Margaret (b. 1916)	103	Turner, Lana (b. 1920)	132
Crawford, Joan (1904-1977)	63	Lollobrigida, Gina (b. 1927)	168		
		Lombard, Carole (1908-1942)	56	Vitti, Monica (b. 1931)	194
Darrieux, Danielle (b. 1917)	127	Loren, Sophia (b. 1934)	164		
Davies, Marion (1897-1961)	28	Loy, Myrna (b. 1905)	60	Weaver, Sigourney (b. 1949)	214
Davis, Bette (b. 1908)	96	Lupino, Ida (b. 1918)	116	West, Mae (1892-1980)	46
Day, Doris (b. 1924)	157			Winger, Debra (b. 1955)	221
De Havilland, Olivia (b. 1916)	80	MacLaine, Shirley (b. 1934)	191	Wong, Anna May (1907-1961)	45
Del Rio, Dolores (1905-1983)	43	Magnani, Anna (1908-1973)	151	Wray, Fay (b. 1907)	42
Deneuve, Catherine (b. 1943)	204	Mangano, Silvana (b. 1930)	167	Wyman, Jane (b. 1914)	157
Dietrich, Marlene (b. 1901)	71	Mansfield, Jayne (1933-1967)	182		
Dunaway, Faye (b. 1941)	207	Monroe, Marilyn (1926-1962)	169	Young, Loretta (b. 1913)	70
Dunne, Irene (b. 1904)	69	Moore, Colleen (b. 1900)	22		
		Moreau, Jeanne (b. 1928)	187		
Farrow, Mia (b. 1945)	206	Morgan, Michèle (b. 1920)	125		
Fonda, Jane (b. 1937)	198	Murray, Mae (1889-1965)	20		
Fontaine, Joan (b. 1917)	115				
Francis, Kay (1905-1968)	54	Neagle, Anna (b. 1904)	103		
		Negri, Pola (b. 1894)	17		
Garbo, Greta (b. 1905)	34	Novak, Kim (b. 1933)	173		
Gardner, Ava (b. 1922)	147				
Garland, Judy (1922-1969)	152	Oberon, Merle (1911-1979)	90		
Garson, Greer (b. 1908)	102	O'Hara, Maureen (b. 1920)	130		
Gaynor, Janet (1906-1984)	42				
Gish, Lillian (b. 1896)	18	Pfeiffer, Michelle (b. 1959)	222		